DATA
COMMUNICATIONS
FOR
PROGRAMMERS

INTERNATIONAL COMPUTER SCIENCE SERIES

Consulting editors **A D McGettrick**
University of Strathclyde

J van Leeuwen
University of Utrecht

DATA COMMUNICATIONS FOR PROGRAMMERS

Michael Purser

Trinity College Dublin

ADDISON-WESLEY
PUBLISHING
COMPANY

Wokingham, England · Reading, Massachusetts · Menlo Park, California
Don Mills, Ontario · Amsterdam · Sydney · Singapore · Tokyo
Madrid · Bogota · Santiago · San Juan

Cover illustration courtesy of Barry Martin, University of Aston.
Photoset by Mid-County Press.
Printed in Finland by Werner Söderström Osakeyhtiö. Member of Finnprint.

British Library Cataloguing in Publication Data

Purser, Michael
  Data communications for programmers.—
  (International computer science series)
  1. Data transmission systems
  I. Title   II. Series
  001.64   TK5105

  ISBN 0-201-12918-3

Library of Congress Cataloging in Publication Data

Purser, Michael, 1937–
  Data communications for programmers.

  (International computer science series)
  Includes index.
  1. Data transmission systems.   2. Electronic digital
computers—Programming.   I. Title.   II. Series.
TK5105.P87   1986   005.71   85-18689
ISBN 0-201-12918-3 (soft)

ABCDEF 89876

Contents

Preface

This book has been written for two reasons: because students of Computer Science and Engineering at Trinity College Dublin repeatedly asked me to provide a suitable text for them; and because, as a designer and programmer of systems software over many years, I have often felt that no adequate book existed in the field of data communications.

Of course there are many books in the field, and good ones too, so what precise gap does this one propose to fill? It is my experience that the public to whom this book is addressed (software practitioners, and students destined to become them) is composed of busy people, intelligent people, who are capable of grasping concepts quickly if they need them, but have no time to study large texts on topics of no immediate relevance to them. For example, the software designer is told that his next project involves a convolutional encoder. He wants to know rapidly: what is a convolutional encoder? Once he has grasped the general idea he can pursue it further in detailed texts if he wishes. He wants to get a rapid, but not too superficial overview of many subjects as he confronts them in his work.

Frequently such a person turns to manufacturers' manuals for general information. Indeed, most software practitioners are educated from such manuals. They themselves are aware of the limitations of manuals tied to one range of hardware or software, and would like to get a wider view of a topic. For example, it is proposed to purchase a time division multiplexer or concentrator. What features should he look for? The manuals state which features are present, not those that are absent.

Another recurring problem, which has become very common with the proliferation of the microprocessor, is the engineer-turned-programmer. He writes programs like chains of relays: A closes, B opens, therefore C trips, etc. It works. But what is acceptable for a program of 400 instructions operating once a minute becomes less and less acceptable as the program size grows and the rate of external events increases. He becomes aware of the difficulty of meeting response times, of the need for relative priorities and the use of interrupts, of the requirement to suspend one activity temporarily in favour of another. Frequently his first encounter with these problems is again in the field of data communications. A real-time executive for multi-tasking is needed. Can he write it himself? Should he buy it, and if so, what features should it have? How does he write protocols under the executive?

To all these people this book is dedicated. It does not attempt to answer all queries, still less is it, I hope, dogmatic. It attempts to make principles plain and leaves it to the reader to decide if he wishes to pursue the topic or not. In particular it avoids, as far as possible, reproducing at length standard specifications which can be referred to at source (CCITT, ISO, IEEE, etc.). However, a glossary is provided at the end, explaining many standard terms in as concise a manner as possible.

A notable omission in this book is the topic of switched networks. This is deliberate. Switching is a non-trivial subject, as any telephone engineer can tell you, whatever computer people may think. A meshed network is a complex structure. There is more to computer networks than packet switching, and end-to-end protocols. Accordingly, switched data networks are reserved for a following book.

Another omission is a discussion of programming languages for data communications. At the risk of offending many readers I maintain (and I am not alone!) that a competent programmer is able to learn and use any language be it Assembler, C, CHILL or Pascal, in a matter of days; and that the difference between languages is of little importance to him. He is more concerned with program structure; and very frequently with run-time efficiency, which (still) often results in the use of Assembler. If a high-level language is used he is more likely to be worried about the efficiency of the implementation of the language on his particular system than with the language itself.

No book is complete without acknowledgements. My thanks, first and foremost, go to students and other young people in Ireland, and indeed in South America, who have encouraged me to write it. I hope they will not be disappointed by the result. Useful comments on the draft were received from Professor Andrew McGettrick and Joe Ettinger, but any errors in the book are of course my own. My thanks to them. Thanks also to my wife and family for their patience while this work was undertaken. Finally, and most importantly, thanks to Helen Smith and Naomi Ohana who typed and retyped the manuscript. Without them nothing would have been produced.

Michael Purser
Trinity College, Dublin

Chapter 1 **Basic concepts**

1.1 Introduction

The need to communicate with a computer over a distance has been recognized for well over 20 years. From humble beginnings, in which a punched tape output from the computer was perhaps fed into a teleprinter for remote reproduction, data communications have grown into a huge industry. Not only do computers use large and complicated teleprocessing software systems, with special front-end processors for handling many communication links, each with their line adaptors, modems and protocols; but the very infrastructure used for communication is computer-based. Communication channels are merged onto common circuits using microprocessor-controlled multiplexers, and traffic is switched in computer-controlled exchanges.

Telecommunications have invaded the field of computers only marginally less thoroughly than computers have invaded telecommunications.

The programmer and the informed user of computers must become familiar with this convergence of telecommunication and information technologies, often referred to as 'telematics'. (The term 'telematics' sometimes is used with a more restricted meaning to denote text-based systems such as Teletex or Videotex.) However, his introduction to the field is all too often as a result of a specific project, using proprietary software and hardware packages on a particular computer. He does not know what is possible or available outside his limited field of experience.

Data communications technology, however, is based on principles more general than that of specific manufacturers' products. There are the general principles for carrying data, commands, timing and other information usually in a single serial bit-stream; the techniques that enable transmission of data securely in the presence of errors on a channel; the design of software that can give fast response to what is frequently high-speed and unsolicited input; the methods of arbitrating the access from independent computers to a common medium.

These and related topics are the subject of this book. It starts from first principles.

1.2 Parallel transmission

Remote communication between computers, or computer-like devices of greater or lesser capabilities, such as terminals, is usually in the form of serial bit-streams.

1

Before considering such communication it is worth while looking at communication *within* computers; that is, when one piece of electronic equipment communicates with another nearby. It will give us some idea of the functions likely to be required for remote communication. It will also highlight some of the problems we are likely to encounter later.

The typical example of internal communication is that of a computer 'bus', or highway, used to link a processor to memory or to the control unit of a peripheral device. On a computer bus communication is parallel, by which is meant that several bits of data are transferred simultaneously between the two units on parallel circuits. The number of parallel circuits, and therefore the number of bits that can be simultaneously transmitted, is the 'width' of the bus, and varies from 8 to as much as 64 in some large machines.

A typical bus structure [1] is illustrated in Fig. 1.1. As can be seen, many devices are attached to it – hence the name. At any time one device usually called the Master is, typically, in control of the bus, and is communicating with another device, the Slave. In simple systems the Master is always the processor. In more complex systems bus mastership may change; for example, if there are peripheral devices capable of controlling the bus on their own (as occurs if Direct Memory Access, or DMA, is supported), or if more than one processor is attached to the bus.

The bus contains more circuits than those used for carrying data bits. These circuits may be divided into categories, as follows.

Addressing   The Master needs to be able to select the Slave with which it wishes to communicate. To do this it puts an address on the Address circuits which is decoded by all potential slaves. Only the specified Slave will respond to the address, i.e. select itself, and partake in the rest of the communication.

The width of the address may be 16, 20, 24, 32 bits, for example. If it is 16 then 65536 distinct addresses may be specified, far greater than the likely number of devices; but if the address selects not only the device but items within a device (e.g. octets in memory) then 16 is a small number. (The word 'octet' is used throughout

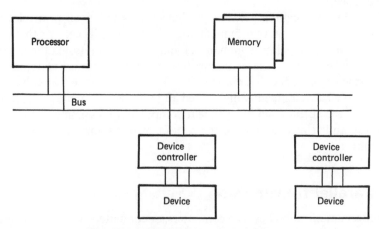

Fig. 1.1   Typical computer parallel bus

this book, rather than 'byte', since it makes it quite clear that a group of 8 bits is indicated.)

Data   These circuits are used to carry the parallel data, and are driven by the Master or Slave, whichever is sending the data. Sometimes two distinct sets of circuits are provided, a set for each direction, thus providing a full-duplex communication path. More usually, the data circuits are bidirectional (that is, capable of transferring data in both directions) but not simultaneously, i.e. a half-duplex path.

Control   The Master needs to be able to tell the Slave what data transfer to perform: a 'Read' (Slave-to-Master) or a 'Write' (Master-to-Slave). These circuits are used to specify this. Additionally they may specify details of the transfer, for example its width. Although there may be 16 data lines maybe only one octet is to be transferred, so only 8 will be used.

Timing   It is not sufficient simply to put Address or Data bits on the bus and assume the receiver will get them. The receiver must be told when that information is valid. Typically the Address and Control lines are asserted by the Master, and later the Data lines by the Master or Slave. This can be done in synchronism with timing pulses on a special circuit of the bus ('on the third pulse the Address lines are valid', 'on the fifth pulse the data lines are valid if the Master is transmitting, or if the Slave is transmitting, then on the sixth pulse'), in which case we have a synchronous bus.

Alternatively an asynchronous bus can be used (see Fig. 1.2). Here, for example, A asserts a 'strobe' pulse X, when the data it sends are valid, and B asserts a response pulse Y when it has read them. A then removes X to show the data are no longer valid, and B removes Y in response to show that it too has finished. Even on a short bus there are propagation delays, so the situation as seen at A (Fig. 1.2a) is different from that seen at B (Fig. 1.2b).

Interrupt   Normally the Master is the central processor and only communicates with a Slave when told by the program it is obeying. However, a device may wish to communicate with the central processor spontaneously, for example as a result of some external event such as a button being pushed, or a transfer (e.g. rewind of a magnetic tape) being completed. Interrupts are used for this. An Interrupt circuit may be controlled by a competent device controller, which sends a pulse on that circuit. The processor's response depends much on its design. This varies from a very basic scheme in which the interrupt forces entry to a program (the interrupt handler) which then interrogates all possible interrupting devices to determine which one caused the interrupt; to sophisticated schemes in which the processor (by hardware logic rather than by software) requests the device to deliver an interrupt 'vector' via the Data circuits. Typically the vector is the address of an interrupt routine peculiar to that device.

Many computers have several interrupt lines, with different devices connected to different ones. The different lines have different priorities, by which is meant that the processor will accept the interrupt only if its own priority (determined by its processor status word) is lower and there are no higher-

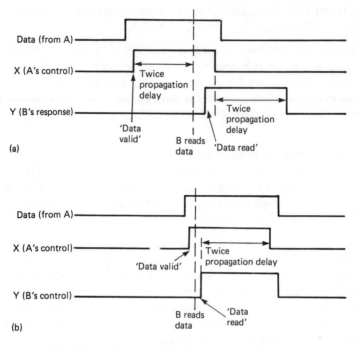

Fig. 1.2 (a) Data transfer from A (as seen at A);
(b) data transfer from A (as seen at B)

priority interrupts. Thus an interrupt signal should not be a pulse, but rather a level which remains asserted by the interrupting device until it is assured that the processor has accepted it.

Arbitration If there can be only one bus Master, there is no need to make provision for changing bus mastership. But if there are potentially several Masters, circuits are required to enable a would-be Master to request mastership and to be granted it. The request on a simple system might go to the normal Master, the processor. On a more complex system, e.g. with several processors, it would go to an Arbitration Unit which decides who the next Master will be. A processor has to ask the Arbitration Unit like any other device. These circuits which carry signals for changing bus mastership are sometimes called Arbitration circuits.

Initialization Frequently a bus contains an initialization line. Despite the nature of the bus, this is usually the only broadcast signal which affects all devices. It is typically asserted by the processor when it first powers up, or when it resets. The signal is then used by each piece of equipment attached to the bus to initialize itself to a known state.

Powerfail Sometimes another broadcast signal is provided so that the processor can signal all devices that it is powering down, deliberately or as a result of a failure. The devices use this signal to power themselves down.

Power   Power itself, in the form of $+5$ V, -12 V, etc., is sometimes distributed to device controllers via the bus.

The above circuits form a sheaf of parallel communication paths, often up to 100 circuits wide or more, which link pieces of equipment, near to each other, together. In serial transmission, there are typically far fewer circuits – perhaps only a single simplex or half-duplex channel – on which to send not only data but also the equivalent of some or all of the above signals, including, perhaps, power. In the following chapters we shall see how some of these facilities are provided by hardware, while others are provided by software, in the form of line procedures, or line disciplines.

1.3 Serial transmission

Serial transmission means the sending of one bit after another along a single channel. Serial transmission offers two advantages over parallel transmission when used over longer distances:

- The problem of how to ensure that all the bits being sent in parallel are received in parallel at the far end is avoided. The difference in propagation times, leading to 'skew' arrival between bits on parallel channels, does not arise if there is only one channel.

- The cost of the link, per bit per second of capacity, is generally cheaper than that obtaining if parallel transmission is used. This reflects the increasing predominance of the circuit cost (often the cost of copper wire) over the transmitter/receiver interface costs at the ends of the circuit, as distance increases. It becomes cheaper to increase the sophistication of the transmitter/receiver pair, thereby achieving a higher throughput capacity, than to look for the same result by adding circuits in parallel.

Data normally exist in a mixture of parallel and serial forms in a computer. For example, a text file is composed of a series of characters which are read serially, but each character is formed of eight parallel bits. If such data are to be sent over a serial channel the whole file must be serialized bit by bit. Typically this is done by sending out bit 0 (the least significant bit), then bits 1, 2, 3, etc., to 7 of the first character; then bits 0, 1, 2, to 7 of the second character; and so forth. (In some computers and codes, e.g. IBM EBCDIC, the most significant bit is sent first.) The rate at which the bits are sent out is called the bit-rate, and is typically measured in bits per second (bps).

Computers have special hardware modules available for this serial transmission. These modules are variously called line adaptors, line control units or line interfaces. For sending, the line adaptor must receive (from an output instruction in a program) an octet, which is then serialized bit by bit and sent out at the required bit-rate, as determined by switches set in the module or by a previous command from a program. The line adaptor must have a means of signalling the program when it is ready to receive another octet for sending.

Normally an interrupt is used for this. Should the program not respond fast enough to this signal, there will be an interval of indeterminate length on the line between the last bit of one octet and the first of the next octet.

The heart of a line adaptor is usually a USART (Universal Synchronous/ Asynchronous Receiver/Transmitter) chip, which performs the serial/parallel conversion [2].

For receiving, the USART shifts in the serial bits from the line into a register, until an octet has been accumulated. It then signals the computer, again usually with an interrupt, to request a program to read the octet (using an input instruction). Should the program not react quickly enough, the octet is likely to be lost by being overwritten by subsequent incoming bits from the line.

Line adaptors are often double-buffered, if they do not offer more sophisticated buffering using Direct Memory Access (DMA) or Silos. Double-buffering (Fig. 1.3) allows the program a complete octet-time to respond to interrupt, e.g. $10^6 \times 8 \div 9600 = 833$ μs, if the bit-rate is 9600 bps as opposed to less than a bit-time, e.g. 104 μs. On output, the bits are sent from the octet in the first transmit buffer. As soon as it is empty it is reloaded from the second transmit buffer and the request interrupt is sent to the computer. On input, the bits are shifted into the first receive buffer. As an octet is accumulated, it is transferred to the second receiver buffer and the interrupt sent to the computer. The computer accesses only the second transmit and receive buffers and has the full octet-time to do so while transfer to/from the line takes place in the first buffers.

A line adaptor in a computer is generally a full-duplex device. This means that it can handle transmission and reception simultaneously. Sometimes this facility is not necessary but one important use for it is when testing. It is very useful when testing teleprocessing programs to be able to feed back the transmitted data into the computer. This can be done easily by looping back the transmit serial line to the receive serial line on a full-duplex line adaptor. It is clear that the technique of *sending* serial data is relatively easy. The line adaptor must

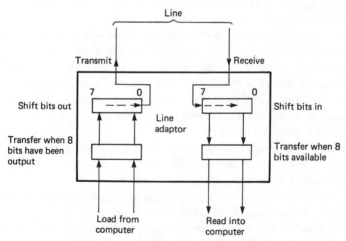

Fig. 1.3   A double-buffered line adaptor

contain, or be supplied with, clocking pulses at the bit-rate, which will be used to shift out the serial bits to the line. If the supply of octets from the program fails, the clocking can be stopped, to start up again when more octets are available. If the interval between stopping and restarting does not contain an integral number of bit-times, we have anisochronous transmission. Alternatively, in isochronous transmission, bits all occur regularly on the clock pulses, with the intervals (if any) between octets containing an integral number of (dummy) bits. In either case, if the channel is capable of carrying only a logical 1 or 0, this interval between octets will be filled by one or other of those values.

These considerations show that the *receiving* of serial data is not nearly so straightforward. Even without the problem of possible intervals between octets, how are we to ensure that the receiver will clock in bits at precisely the same rate as, and in the correct phase with, the remote sender? If the bits are a succession like 10101010, etc., then clearly they identify themselves and effectively carry the clock signal with them: but what of a series of continuous logical ones or zeros? And even if we can identify and extract each bit from the continuous received stream, how do we know where octets begin and end in that stream? If, in addition, we consider possible intervals between octets in the incoming stream, how do we distinguish the dummy bits filling the interval from the real bits of the octets? And if transmission is anisochronous, how do we keep the clock in the receiver in synchronism with the remote clock in the sender? The problem is similar to that addressed by the timing circuits of the parallel bus discussed earlier. Timing signals of some sort are required to tell the receiver when to look at the incoming information.

1.4 Stop-Start or asynchronous transmission

A solution to this problem has existed for a very long time in the field of telegraphy and telex. In this case the octets are characters; for example, coded in 5 bits using the IA2 code or coded in 7 bits using the IA5 code [3] – which is equivalent to ISO-7 or ASCII. Each character is preceded by a Start bit and followed, typically, by 1, $1\frac{1}{2}$ or 2 Stop bits. Various terms are used to designate the polarity of the bits. These are:

Start = Space = A = Logical 0

Stop = Mark = Z = Logical 1

The complete format for a 7-bit character plus one parity bit, with one Start and two Stop bits is illustrated in Fig. 1.4. Figure 1.5 shows the letter X in IA5 with odd parity in the same format. It should be noted that on the V24 interface (Chapter 2) the actual voltage levels (defined for example by V28) are such that

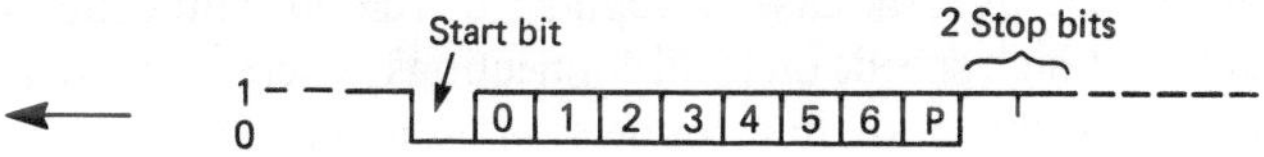

Fig. 1.4 Start-stop transmission

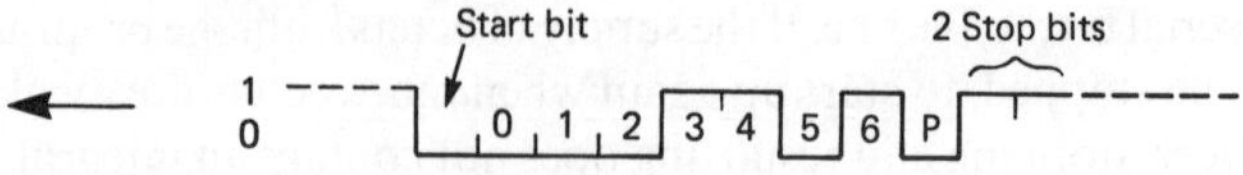

Fig. 1.5 The letter X transmitted

logical 1 is negative and logical 0 positive so, when seen on oscilloscope, Figs. 1.4 and 1.5 would appear upside down. Moreover, since the least significant bit is assumed as transmitted first, it will appear on the left, so the character is apparently back to front as well as upside down.

The transmitting asynchronous line adaptor is responsible for adding the initial Start and final Stop bits to the character supplied from the computer and often generates the Parity bit. As in the case of the bit-rate, the choice of the parameters (1, $1\frac{1}{2}$ or 2 Stop bits; Even, Odd, Zero, One or No Parity) is selected either by switches on the module or by a command to the module from the computer. Unless operating with electromechanical devices or single-buffered line adaptors which may require a longer intercharacter pause, one Stop bit is often used; although two Stop bits may be necessary on connections subject to much distortion.

In Europe, the receiving asynchronous line adaptor is normally in the idle state receiving a continuous Mark, and awaiting the transition to Space which indicates the beginning of a Start bit. (This convention is reversed in the USA.) As soon as this transition occurs a clock is started which is used to sample the rest of the Start bit. Typically, five or seven samples per bit are made, and the logic decides whether a 1 or a 0 has been received, according to which value predominates in the sample. If a proper Start bit is identified, the samples continue in a similar fashion for the bits that make up the character and the Stop bits. If a proper Start bit is not found, the search for it begins again. If the Stop bits are found to be Space, the receiving line adaptor will normally signal a Break character or an error to the computer. The receiving line adaptor must be set up to read at the same bit-rate as the sender, and to expect the same number of Stop bits and parity polarity. However, its clock does not have to be exactly synchronized with the sender's; it has only to ensure that any difference in the two clock rates produces no problems over the duration of the $8 + 3$ bits, and its phase is determined by the beginning of the received Start bit. Moreover the character itself is clearly identifiable in its Stop-Start envelope.

This form of serial transmission is commonly called Stop-Start or Asynchronous transmission, although it should properly be called Anisochronous. Its major disadvantage is that it requires a Start and at least one Stop bit per character. In the case of an 8-level (data bits), 11-unit (total bits) code this means that 3 bits in 11, or 27% of capacity is lost. This is unacceptable when channel capacity is expensive, as is the case for high-speed remote connections. However, at low speeds, or at high speeds on local connections (where no carrier equipment is necessary but a direct digital connection is made between terminal and computer), asynchronous communication is normal. Synchronous (or isochronous) transmission, which is designed to overcome the limitations of asynchronous transmission, is discussed in Chapter 3.

The character-oriented format of asynchronous transmission obviously suits terminals which handle characters, such as teleprinters, Visual Display Units (VDUs) composed of screens and keyboards, etc. Such terminals are normally used in half-duplex mode, conversations being alternate between the user and the computer with only one transmitting at a time. In this case a full-duplex channel linking computer and terminal may not be necessary, even though both the terminal and the computer's line adaptor may be capable of full-duplex working. Indeed, many terminals have a switch labelled Full-Duplex/Half-Duplex. If half-duplex is selected, data entered at the keyboard will appear on the presentation unit (screen or printer), and reception from the remote computer may be locked out while the keyboard is in use. Conversely, the keyboard may be locked to prevent transmission when reception is in progress. However, even though conversations are basically half-duplex, there are often good reasons for requiring a full-duplex channel. These are:

- It may be desirable to be able to interrupt an incoming flow of data, e.g. an unwanted printout at a terminal.

- It may be required to use 'remote echo' in which the character entered at the keyboard is echoed back to the presentation unit by the remote computer. This confirms its reception and also gives the possibility of altering and inserting characters in the echoed data stream. This is particularly useful for controlling the formatted display on a screen, since the computer can control the layout without obliging the user to type extra Carriage Return, Line Feed, Tabulation or Cursor Control characters.

- When modems (see Chapter 2) are used, a full-duplex channel can significantly reduce the time it takes to turn around a line from receiving to transmitting and vice versa.

A full-duplex channel can often be achieved by allocating half the bandwidth available on a single physical circuit to each of the two directions. Alternatively, two completely separate physical circuits may be provided, one for each direction. In telephone parlance, two separate physical circuits are often called a 4-wire connection. A 4-wire connection is always full-duplex. A 2-wire connection (by analogy with a 2-wire local telephone loop) is half-duplex or full-duplex depending on how the bandwidth is used. Generally speaking, only low-speed transmission can be full-duplex on a 2-wire connection.

Mention has been made of a parity bit per character. This bit, of course, is made 1 or 0 to ensure that the total number of 1s in the character is even or odd, as required. On reception, the parity of the character is checked, and if it is incorrect the character or the message is rejected. Sometimes this eighth bit is always made 1 ('forced-eight') or always 0. For in-house connections it is probably best omitted. The redundancy of ordinary English text, as opposed to numbers, is such that a single corrupted character is frequently correctable by eye on output, while corrupted characters on input will probably cause some validation routine in the computer to fail, and advise the user, even if no parity is used. In the case of remote connections, where the probability of corrupting bits is higher, parity checks are more useful. In practice, however, many computer systems ignore the parity bits on asynchronous lines but nevertheless include the useless bit in the character's format, using up line capacity.

1.5 Summary

Remote serial transmission must at least include techniques enabling a receiver to recognize received bits and octets for what they are; i.e. rules for ensuring that the received data are strobed at the right frequency and phase. The technique of start-stop transmission achieves this, albeit in a not very efficient manner. We must now consider how the data are to be conveyed physically between transmitter and receiver.

References

1. Three well known examples of parallel buses are:
    i) 'Unibus' Digital Equipment Corporation, Maynard, Massachusetts,
    ii) 'Multibus' IEEE P-796,
    iii) 'S-100 Bus' Altair.

2. Examples of USARTs are given by the '8274 Multi-protocol serial controller' Intel Corporation; 'Z 8530 SCC' Zilog; 'Multi-protocol Communications Controller' Signetics; 'MC 6852' Motorola.

3. The IA5 alphabet is to be found in Recommendation V5 of *Vol. VIII* of the CCITT publications (*Red Book*). IA2 is in *Vol. VII* (*Series S*).

Chapter 2 **Remote serial transmission**

2.1 The physical connection

It has been assumed that it is possible to send the serial data from one line adaptor to another remote one. This requires a transmission medium and, usually, some device at the sending end to transform the digital data received from the line adaptor into a form which can be carried by the medium. A similar device at the receiving end performs the reverse process (Fig. 2.1). In theory, the medium could be almost anything: radio carrier wave, optical carrier, a suitable cable, etc. In practice, there are practical, legal and technical restrictions.

The practical problem is that of providing the medium. You cannot lay cables across other people's property, nor across water, etc., without considerable difficulties. A line-of-sight optical link may be easier to establish, but it is liable, as radio links certainly are, to official regulations. In most countries the common or licensed communications carriers, which in Europe are usually referred to as the PTTs (although some are private, some are semi-state companies), have very considerable legal powers to stop people installing their own communication circuits. These powers are certain to be used if there is any possibility of 'third parties' being allowed to use such a 'private' communication circuit. In practice, private circuits are feasible options only within a restricted area such as a university campus or a large industrial complex, or where the user has extensive physical routes of his own. Such users could be railway companies, which can lay cable along their tracks; or electrical utility companies, which can transmit information over the high-tension cables using the technique of Power Line Carrier; or perhaps the military.

The principal technical restriction on using a long-distance electrical circuit is that direct digital signalling at the levels of power supplied by most line adaptors does not work at a distance over a few hundred metres. The higher the bit-rate, the shorter the feasible distance. Connecting the transmit line of one adaptor to the receive line of the other, and vice versa, via a pair of wires is a practical option only over short distances, where one has permission to lay the wires.

All this implies that in the vast majority of cases the user is obliged to use circuits supplied by the licensed common carriers, the PTTs, and to employ the interfacing devices mentioned in the first paragraph to transform his low-powered digital signals to/from a form which can be carried on the circuit he is using. These interfacing devices are known as Data Circuit-terminating

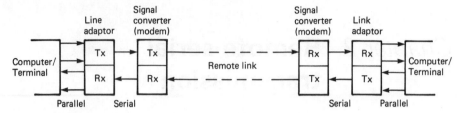

Fig. 2.1 Remote serial transmission

Equipment, or DCEs. A DCE can be supplied by the provider of the circuit, the PTT or a commercial supplier, depending on local regulations. Standard interfaces have been defined by CCITT which specify the electrical characteristics, significance and use of the signals which must unite a line adaptor and the DCE [1]. (CCITT, Comité Consultatif International de Télégraphie et Téléphonie, a body representing most of the suppliers of telecommunications services in the world, is part of the International Telecommunications Union with headquarters in Geneva. A large number of CCITT Recommendations are paralleled by EIA standards in the USA; see the References at the end of the chapter.)

In CCITT parlance the line adaptor and connected computer or terminal are all subsumed in the term Data Terminal Equipment, or DTE. Manufacturers of computers and terminals (DTEs) will nearly always ensure that their equipment is compatible with one of these standard interfaces, for example the V24 interface which is discussed below. As a consequence, suppliers of equipment for private circuits, such as optical links, will arrange that their equipment also uses an internationally agreed interface so that it can be connected to readily available DTEs.

2.1.1 Networks for data transmission supplied by the PTTs

The PTTs essentially supply switched services. In the case of switched circuits, the circuit which one leases from the PTT is a circuit to the local exchange. This means that the DTE must have a means of establishing and clearing a circuit across the switched network, as well as using it, if communication with a remote DTE is to be possible. Call set-up, as it is named, involves 'selecting' the remote DTE – a procedure analogous to dialling with the telephone. Clearing a call is usually a simpler procedure than setting it up. The PTTs' tariffs have traditionally been based on the duration and distance of calls, rather than on the amount of information transferred during the call, although this is not so for the newer packet-switched services.

Users who wish to transfer large volumes of data regularly between two fixed DTEs may find it more convenient and cheaper to lease a permanent circuit, rather than go through the call set-up procedure each time data are to be sent. Such a permanent circuit is provided by 'patching-through' circuits in the exchanges of the PTT's network. The switching mechanism is bypassed, and a permanent circuit is established between the two DTEs via the exchanges and the

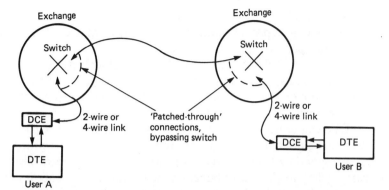

Fig. 2.2 A leased line

trunk circuits (Fig. 2.2). Such a permanent circuit is usually called a 'leased line'. The user typically pays a quarterly rental which depends on the distance between the two DTEs. He can then make any use he likes of his circuit, apart from offering it to third parties. (On packet-switched networks leasees of Permanent Virtual Circuits – the equivalent of leased lines – must still pay volume charges.)

The PTTs offer three main types of networks which may be used for data transmission. The three types are:

- telex, or telex-like circuit-switched networks,
- the telephone network,
- packed-switched data networks.

These networks are often more distinguished by the facilities and interfaces they offer to the user than by their internal construction. In fact modern tele-communications networks use a very large variety of techniques internally. Transmission can be over a traditional pair of telephone wires; multipair cables; using Frequency Division Multiplexing over coaxial cable or microwave radio link; via satellite; using digital (PCM) time division multiplexing over telephone pairs or optical fibre connections; etc. Switching can be done using the old-fashioned electromechanical Strowger, crossbar, or all digital equipment; with a computer analysing the selection (dialled) requests and driving the mechanical switch to make the connections; with a computer performing the switching as an internal (software) function; etc. Telex and packet-switched networks often use the circuits of the telephone network to link their exchanges. Access to a packet-switched network may be available via the telex or telephone network. The interdependence of the PTTs' services is great, and the real distinction is perhaps between the bearer circuits and the services provided on them, rather than between the traditionally identified 'networks'.

Both telex and telephone networks are circuit-switched networks. A circuit-switched network is one in which a through connection between DTEs is established and maintained for the duration of a call. This connection has a known capacity for carrying traffic and is exclusively available to the DTEs involved as long as the call exists – even if they may temporarily be transmitting nothing. Circuit-switched networks effectively couple remote equipment which must be compatible in respect of speed (bit-rate), data format, etc. The network transfers data transparently.

By contrast, in a packet-switched network, data are blocked into 'packets' for sending between DTEs, and packets from many different conversations are interleaved on common shared circuits. Circuits are used more efficiently in this technique since other conversations can take advantage of the unused capacity when a DTE is temporarily silent. Another advantage is that, since packets are accumulated and stored at each node, or exchange, and then forwarded to the next one, corresponding DTEs need not operate at the same speed. The 'store-and-forward' technique provides a buffer on the line, as well as scope for format conversions. An obvious disadvantage of package switching is that when traffic becomes heavy performance is likely to degrade, since there will be competition for the shared capacity of the circuits, and indeed of the nodes.

Telex-like networks as seen by the user are briefly discussed here, and the use of the telephone network for data transmission is handled at more length. Proper data networks (such as packet-switched networks), in which calls are set up by computer rather than manually, are outside the scope of this book, which is essentially concerned with non-switched services. However, in Chapter 6 the X.25 protocol used for interfacing to packet-switched networks is briefly presented, since it provides a familiar example of multiplexing many channels on a single physical circuit.

2.1.2 Telex-like networks

The telex network originally evolved to allow the transmission of characters in start-stop format using digital signalling at low speeds, e.g. 50 bps, with a 5-bit code. The representation of data could be, for example, logical $1 = -80$ V, logical $0 = +80$ V. Pulse repeaters in the network ensured that attenuation was kept within acceptable limits. Terminals, in the form of teleprinters, are directly connected onto a telex exchange line. To allow other types of DTE to access the network an appropriate DCE is needed. Typically a telegraph adaptor is used. This is a device providing a standard V24 interface (see Section 2.2.3) so that DTEs can readily connect to it on one side, and on the other it is attached directly onto the 2- or 4-wire telex line. The telegraph adaptor will contain its own power supply to drive the 80 V telex line. If a switched connection is required it would typically be set up using the ordinary telex procedures on a teleprinter, switching the exchange line over manually to the telegraph adaptor, and hence to the DTE, when the call set-up is complete (Fig. 2.3). Alternatively, systems for automatic switchover and automatic selection are possible, in which the computer essentially emulates the manual procedure. Half-duplex operation is usual on switched connections, but a full-duplex leased line is possible.

Telex traffic is in fact often transmitted on carrier circuits, and as such could operate at higher speeds provided that there are no purely 80 V digital sections in the path. Typically these sections are in the local line from DCE to exchange. In some countries the telex network has been upgraded by extending carrier or

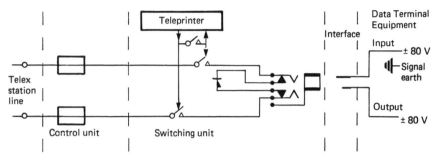

Fig. 2.3   A telex interface

similar facilities to the DCE, and the interface offered to the user is either V24-compatible or the newer X20 (for start-stop transmission) or X21 (for synchronous transmission), or their interim versions X20 bis, X21 bis. These newer X-interfaces include, among other features, specific procedures for selecting the remote DTE, and so properly belong to real data networks [2].

2.2 Data transmission via the telephone network

In most countries of the world the principal medium for remote data transmission is still the telephone network. The telephone network is extensive, often reaching very remote areas; and it is very dense in centres of population. Given that it is rarely practicable or permitted to provide one's own transmission medium, the most natural choice, when selecting a circuit to lease from the PTT, is a telephone circuit. With few exceptions, the telephone network has a far higher attainable bit-rate, compared with the 50 bps or so of the telex network. This gives faster responses to interactive users. It also means a shorter time for the transfer of a given volume of data; and, since duration charges for dial-up connections are similar on the telephone and telex networks, the cost is significantly lower. Leased lines, too, on the telephone network are more attractive because of their very much higher capacity: lines are usually rented by persons or organizations with large volumes of data to transfer.

2.2.1 The need for modems

The big problem with the telephone network is that it was never designed to carry digital data. It was built to carry audio traffic, which consists of analogue signals in the range 0–20 000 cycles per second (20 kHz). In practice, the human voice can be safely restricted to 0–4 kHz without any loss of intelligibility. Accordingly, the carrier circuits employed between telephone exchanges confine the bandwidth of voice channels to this range, using the techniques of Frequency Division Multiplexing (FDM) or Pulse Code Modulation (PCM). Thus a special type of DCE, known as a modem (an abbreviation of modulator/demodulator) is required to connect DTEs to telephone circuits. The essential function of a

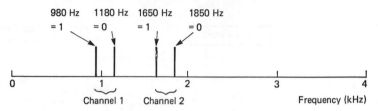

Fig. 2.4 V21 modem FSK modulation

modem is the conversion of digital data for transmission into analogue waveforms in the 0–4 kHz bandwidth, and the reverse process on reception.

Figure 2.4 illustrates the modulation technique employed by the simplest type of modem, namely one compatible with CCITT Recommendation V21 [1]. This modem provides a full-duplex circuit on a 2-wire connection by allocating distinct portions of the bandwidth to each direction. It is important to realize that the analogue signals are voltages *between* the two wires of a 2-wire pair. The two logically separated channels provided by the V21 modem are distinguished by their *frequencies*. The separate frequencies can appear simultaneously on the 2-wire circuit. On Channel 1, a logical 1 received from the DTE is converted into a sinusoidal waveform of 980 Hz, which lasts for the duration of the logical 1 pulse. A logical 0 is converted into 1180 Hz. On Channel 2, a logical 1 is represented by 1650 Hz, logical 0 by 1850 Hz. A convention establishes that, on a switched connection, the caller is allocated Channel 1 for transmission and Channel 2 for reception; so the modem at the called DTE receives on Channel 1 and transmits on Channel 2.

This general technique of switching on or off oscillators in accordance with the digital bit-stream is known as Frequency Shift Keying (FSK). It can be used at low data rates. In the particular case of the frequencies employed in the V21 modem, the technique works well up to 300 bps. This is very crudely equivalent to a sinusoidal modulation of up to 150 Hz (depending on the sequence of logical 1s and 0s) which produces the approximate spectrum of Fig. 2.5.

It is clear that a higher bit-rate, which would flatten the curves shown, would make the discrimination between 1s and 0s at the receiving modem problematical. It would also cause confusion between the two channels, given that the receiver in the modem must be sensitive to a much lower power than that sent out by the transmitter, so that it might pick up the 'tail' of its own transmitted output on the same 2-wire loop.

Modems handling start-stop data usually use the FSK technique and are generally called asynchronous modems. They contain no inherent clocking

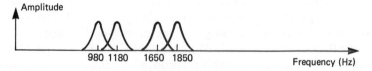

Fig. 2.5 V21 modem modulation in practice

mechanism and are unaware of the bit-rate. The receiving modem turns analogue signals into digital bits, but leaves the identification of the bits to the line adaptor. The modem will work at any bit-rate up to a certain maximum, and the data will be successfully received if the two line adaptors are set to that same rate. The V23 modem, which works at 600 or 1200 bps, also uses the FSK technique.

We shall return to discuss more powerful modems in Chapter 3. Meanwhile, we shall examine some further characteristics of the telephone network when used for data.

2.2.2 Characteristics of telephone circuits for data

The local 2-wire loop between a telephone handset, or a modem, and the exchange may have a very wide bandwidth. As we have seen, this bandwidth may be artificially restricted to 4 kHz on the inter-exchange sections of a given circuit to fit as many voice channels as possible onto the inter-exchange trunk. Figure 2.6 illustrates the FDM technique for what is known as a Group of 12 circuits. Each voice channel has a carrier frequency (like in radio) which is modulated by the voice signal it carries. A coaxial circuit, for example, can support many simultaneous carriers, distinguished by their separate frequencies. Each channel will require a modulator to modulate the carrier with the voice signal, and filter and demodulator to extract the voice signal on reception.

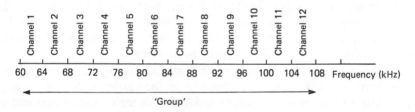

Fig. 2.6   A group of 12 voice channels

It will be appreciated that the existence of amplifiers and filters in these FDM units makes a circuit unidirectional. To enable even the half-duplex traffic required for voice, these carrier portions of the network require separate independent circuits for each direction. In other words, most of the telephone network, excluding the local loop, is inherently full-duplex. It is as though two pairs of wires, one for each direction, linked the two exchanges local to each of the two communicating DTEs (Fig. 2.7). If the connection is a leased line, it is generally a simple matter to extend this '4-wire' circuit by providing a second loop to each DCE from their local exchanges. A genuine full-duplex circuit now exists, and the transmitter of the modem will be on a completely separate circuit to its own receiver. Each direction has the full 4 kHz bandwidth available to it (Fig. 2.8).

It is possible that a connection uses a circuit which includes no carrier section. Two wires effectively connect the two modems, and maybe a bandwidth

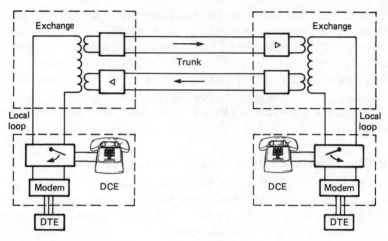

Fig. 2.7   2-wire to 4-wire conversion

much wider than 4 kHz is available to them for communication. If such a connection has been made by dialling, it is impossible to know what type of circuit has been obtained, so its characteristics cannot be exploited. It must be assumed that the bandwidth is 4 kHz, so standard modems are used. If, on the other hand, the connection is a leased line, its nature can be verified. If it is a pure 'wire' connection, whether 2-wire or 4-wire, with no carrier element, then baseband modems can be used to exploit the wider bandwidth. These modems are, typically, cheap and uncomplicated, and offer speeds up to and exceeding those available with sophisticated modems on normal connections.

It has been stated that the bandwidth available on a typical telephone circuit is restricted to 4 kHz, essentially because of the carrier techniques used. In practice, the restriction is more severe, and further distortions are introduced into

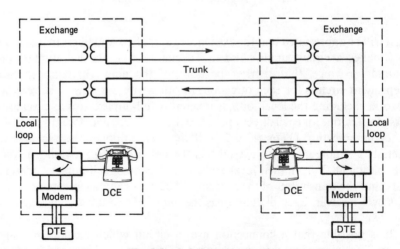

Fig. 2.8   A full 4-wire circuit

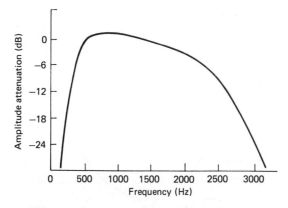

Fig. 2.9   Relative amplitude attenuation on a voice circuit

the transmitted waveforms by the filters and amplifiers of the carrier equipment. Figure 2.9 shows the attenuation of amplitude as a function of the frequency encountered at the receiving end of a typical voice circuit. (Attenuation is measured in dB, with respect to the attenuation at 1000 Hz. The unit of measurement for the relative power of signal A with respect to signal B is defined as $10 \log_{10} (P_A/P_B)$, where P_A and P_B are the powers of signals A and B. If A, B are sinusoidal waveforms, then the powers are proportional to the square of the amplitudes A_A, A_B. For example, if $A_A = A_B/2$ then the attenuation (power loss) $= 10 \log_{10} (1/4) = -10 \log_0 4 = -6$ dB. It will be appreciated from Fig. 2.9 that the effective bandwidth is about 3 kHz, between 0.3 and 3.4 kHz, because of the heavy attenuation at the extremes of the bandwidth.)

Figure 2.10 shows what is known as Relative Group Delay on a typical phone circuit. It indicates the relative delay (in ms) of any frequency component with respect to that of minimum delay, typically around 1800 Hz. Clearly total delay is a function of the propagation time, and hence the distance, between transmitter and receiver. Total delay affects response time, but relative group delay, as illustrated, deforms waveforms. It will be seen that delays of 2–3 ms between different parts of the spectrum which might be used to encode a single digital bit are possible. When we consider that modems operate at bit-rates of several thousand per second, in which a bit lasts less than 1 ms, it is clear that the succeeding bits will be 'smeared' into each other unless the waveform used to represent them is confined to a narrow bandwidth where the group delay curve is 'flat'.

(It should be noted that certain long lines composed of telephone pairs, rather than channels on a carrier, are 'loaded' with inductive coils to improve their characteristics. These 'loaded lines' have quite different attenuation and group delay graphs.)

Relative attenuation and group delay cause the most serious distortions of the waveforms sent from one modem to another. One method of minimizing the distortions is to ensure that a circuit is provided which has certain guaranteed characteristics. For example, one might insist that attenuation and group delay

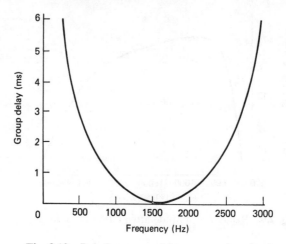

Fig. 2.10 Relative group delay on a voice circuit

lie outside the shaded rectangular areas of Fig. 2.11. The areas, in fact, correspond to the guaranteed features of a leased line 'with C2 conditioning' as applicable in the USA. In Europe, CCITT standards, implemented in a similar way, apply. A CCITT M1040 grade line corresponds to a normal telephone circuit. A CCITT M1020 grade line is conditioned to a standard similar to C2 in the USA. Such conditioning can apply only to leased lines, since it implies adjusting amplifiers and filters along the path of the circuit. This is done manually when the user first receives his circuit, and should be checked again at regular intervals. An alternative approach is to accept the distortions on the line and compensate for them in the modems. This is known as equalization. Essentially, equalization aims to 'flatten' the relative attenuation and group delay curves in the centre of the bandwidth by amplifying the fringe frequencies, and artificially delaying the central ones – see Fig. 2.12. The method whereby this is done is discussed in Chapter 3.

Attenuation and group delay are not the only problems on a telephone circuit. Other sources of disruption are frequency translation, phase jitter, non-linear and harmonic distortion, background and impulsive noise, crosstalk and echo. Frequency translation, in which a frequency component is shifted a few hertz; phase jitter, in which the phase of a waveform jumps randomly; non-linear and harmonic distortions usually have their source in incorrectly operating carrier equipment in the network. Background noise on a telephone circuit is usually -50 dBm (0 dBm $= 1$ mW), which is to be compared with a typical signal strength at the transmitter of -5 to -10 dBm, and 16 to 20 dBm lower at the receiver. Thus, at the receiver a signal-to-noise (S/N) ratio of 20–40 dB is to be expected. A lower figure, due to higher background noise, is likely to cause problems at the limits of the bandwidth. In particular, impulsive noise due to the operation of electromechanical equipment in exchanges can produce sudden high noise levels which cause errors in reception. Impulsive noise is much more serious on dial-up than on leased connections. Crosstalk, in which signals are picked

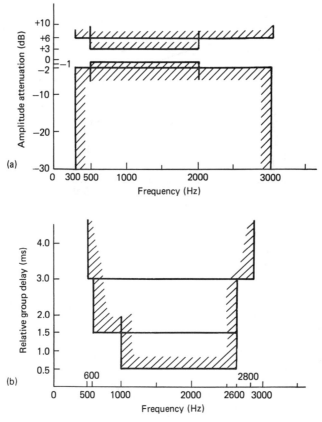

Fig. 2.11 (a) C2 conditioning of attenuation;
(b) C2 conditioning of delay

up from neighbouring circuits, can be caused by excessive power levels on a circuit, and again obscures the real data signals on any circuit on which it is induced.

A major problem with 2-wire dial-up connections can be caused by echo. The principal cause of echo is a mismatch in the equipment for converting from 4-wire to 2-wire operation on dial-up calls using carrier circuits. 'Talker echo' is when a speaker hears his own voice echoed back from the far end (Fig. 2.13). 'Listener echo' results in double reception of a message (Fig. 2.14). On voice connections over long distances echo suppressors are used to eliminate this nuisance. The suppressor closes the reverse channel as long as speech continues in the forward direction. When the echo suppressor detects a pause in the speech and the start of the reply, it will switch over to allow conversation in the reverse direction. This 'turnaround' time is typically 100 ms.

Data traffic on telephone circuits requires frequent reverse messages to confirm its arrival at the far end. If an echo suppressor is in use on the circuit, the time wasted in turning round the suppressor to operate in the reverse direction

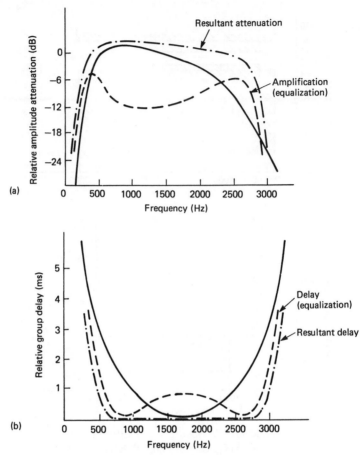

Fig. 2.12   (a) Compensating for relative attenuation;
(b) compensating for relative group delay

causes a severe reduction in throughput. Consequently, on 2-wire circuits used
for data transmission, echo suppressors, if present, must be disabled. This can be
achieved by sending an appropriate tone of 2100 Hz for 400 ms, followed by data.
The suppressor remains disabled as long as this data flow continues without a
break. Some modems exploit this facility, emitting the 2100 Hz tone at suitable
moments in their output waveform, thereby maintaining the echo suppressor
permanently disabled and eliminating the suppressor's turnaround delay. The

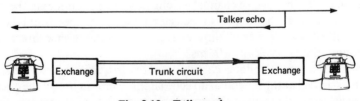

Fig. 2.13   Talker echo

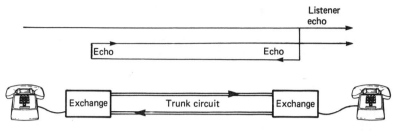

Fig. 2.14   Listener echo

need for this capability in a modem obviously depends on whether an echo suppressor is in the circuit or not. In some countries echo suppressors are potentially in any dial-up circuit, since it could be part of a long-distance call where suppression of voice echo is desirable. In other lands, only international calls are likely to encounter echo suppressors.

The absence of echo suppression from a 2-wire circuit, either because no suppressor is present or because it is disabled, eliminates the turnaround delay associated with it. It does, however, leave the echo! Such echo is a genuine data signal and it is hardly possible to eliminate it by filtering, although it should be heavily attenuated with respect to the real signal. This 'noise' due to echo is often the limiting factor on the performance that can be achieved on a 2-wire data call.

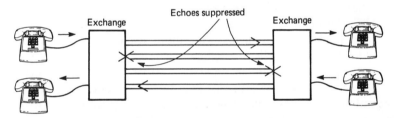

Fig. 2.15   Dual-dial FDX circuit

In the case of leased lines, which, as explained above, are usually 4-wire circuits created by extending the full-duplex trunk network out to the local loops, echo suppressors are not relevant and would not be included in the circuit. Alternatively, if a dual-dial call is made involving the setting up of two 2-wire paths, at double the cost (Fig. 2.15), each circuit can have echo suppressors permanently enabled, since each path is unidirectional. In both cases the echo itself does not exist, and this is another reason why, on such circuits, higher data rates can be achieved using more sophisticated modems.

2.2.3 The V24 modem interface

The existence of a standard serial interface between modem and line adaptor has been mentioned already. This interface is known by its CCITT Recommendation No. V24 [1], and is almost the same as the EIA RS232-C interface used in the USA. (The V24 interface is a logical interface applicable to underlying electrical

Table 2.1 Basic V24 interface

Circuit	Direction	Pin No.	Name
	DTE DCE		
101	←——→	1	Protective Earth
102	←——→	7	Signal Earth
103	——→	2	Transmitted Data
104	←——	3	Received Data
105	——→	4	Request to Send
106	←——	5	Ready for Sending
107	←——	6	Data Set (Modem) Ready
108/1 ⎫ 108/2 ⎬	——→	20	⎧ Connect Data Set to Line ⎨ Data Terminal Ready
109	←——	8	Data Carrier Detect
125	←——	22	Ringing Indicator

interfaces V28, V10 or V11 (see Section 2.2.5), whereas RS232-C is a logical and electrical specification.)

The V24 Recommendation includes a large number of circuits identified by function, name and number, each of which represents a pin on the 25-pin standard connector. However, the allocation of circuit to pin is in fact part of an ISO (International Standards Organization) specification, ISO 2110 [3], rather than CCITT. Many of the circuits are rarely used, and some are applicable only to synchronous modems or modems with more elaborate facilities such as secondary backward channels. Accordingly, a subset of the circuits has been selected in Table 2.1 to simplify presentation. Further circuits will be introduced when necessary in the text. A fuller list is to be found in the Appendix.

The simplest way of explaining the use of the circuits in Table 2.1 is to discuss the example of what happens when a user dials a typical time-sharing computer using the V21 FSK modem already mentioned. To do this, it is first necessary to say a word about the telephone/modem switching arrangements. Essentially the connection is made between two telephones, one being the caller's, the other being located beside the called computer. To send data, it is necessary to switch the modems onto the line, rather than the telephone handsets (Fig. 2.16). A variety of ways exists for doing this. In our case we shall assume that the modem at the computer will be connected to line using the signals on the V24 interface, while the caller's switchover from phone to modem (data) will be manual, using a push button. The actual contacts switched are located in a box labelled Data Access Arrangement (DAA), which may be free-standing, or incorporated into the modem or telephone. The manual switch could be on the telephone, the DAA box, or the modem.

The call starts (Fig. 2.17) with the caller dialling the number of the telephone at the computer. This will cause it to ring, and besides operating the bell, a signal from the phone will be fed back through the DAA to the modem to activate Circuit 125 on the V24 interface. Typically, this will set a status bit in the line

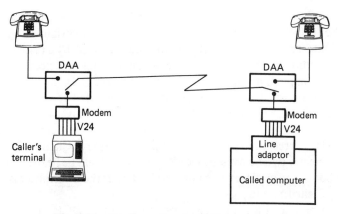

Fig. 2.16 Configuration for calling a computer

adaptor and be used to cause an interrupt to the computer to draw attention to an incoming call. The next step is to switch the modem to line using Circuit 108. This can be done in one of two ways. Variant 108/1 (which does not have an RS232-C equivalent) may be used, in which case 108 is asserted by the program via the line adaptor (DTE) and signifies 'Connect Data Set (Modem) to Line'. The line is

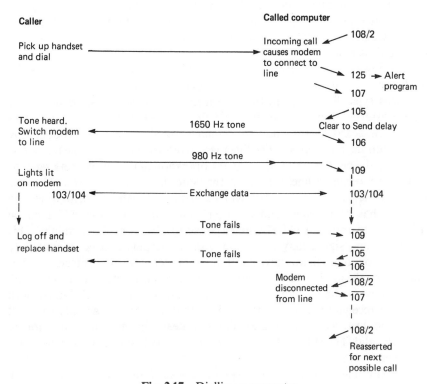

Fig. 2.17 Dialling a computer

switched from the phone to the modem and, when switching is complete, Circuit 107 'Data Set (Modem) Ready' is asserted. Alternatively, variant 108/2 is used, and called 'Data Terminal Ready'. If this is already asserted, by a prior command from the program, at the time that the incoming call is detected, then the switchover will happen at once, followed by assertion of 107.

When the program in the computer detects 107 asserted, it will command the line adaptor to assert Circuit 105 'Request to Send'. This will switch on the modem's transmitter, which, in the case of the V21 modem, will emit a continuous tone of 1650 Hz corresponding to the idle 'marking' state of Channel 2. This note is A♭ (A flat), nearly two octaves above Concert A, and will be heard by the caller on his telephone. The modem will signal the DTE that the transmitter is on using Circuit 106 'Clear to Send'.

The delay between the DTE's assertion of 105 and the DCE's assertion of 106 is commonly referred to as the Ready for Sending or the Clear to Send (or C2S or CTS) Delay. It represents in our case the time it takes the transmitter to reach full power plus an allowed time for the remote modem receiver to lock into the signal. The delay could, with another modem, also include allowances for equalization to take place, or for an echo suppressor to turn itself around (see Section 2.2.2). In particular, if the circuit were half-duplex (unlike our illustration), this CTS Delay would apply every time the modem and DTE turned round from receiving to sending. With a full-duplex circuit the CTS Delay applies only when a conversation is initiated, since the transmitter of the modem can remain on throughout the conversation. This is the main reason why users will request a full-duplex leased line, rather than a half-duplex (2-wire) one, even although their use of the circuit is half-duplex.

Returning to our example, using a V21 modem, when the user hears the 1650 Hz tone, he will operate the 'Data' button to connect the modem to line. The effect of this, typically, is to route the line through to the modem as though 108/1 had been asserted, but without disconnecting the telephone. In fact, the data traffic can be heard on the phone and interesting effects can be produced by whistling into the mouthpiece. The line may be returned finally to the telephone by replacing the handset. Alternatively, the operation of the button may serve to connect the modem to line, subject to the condition that the user's DTE has asserted 108/2. In either case 107 will be asserted by the modem when the connection has been made, and the user's modem transmitter will then be switched on, to transmit 980 Hz, in response to 105 from the terminal. This Request to Send signal may be strapped in the terminal to be permanently asserted, although it will not have effect in the modem until 107 is true. The 106 response from the modem may or may not have a physical effect on the terminal. It will, however, usually light a control lamp on the modem. Provided both modems are receiving the transmitted 1650 or 980 Hz from the far ends, they will signal Carrier Detect on 109. To the DTEs, this means that any incoming data are potentially valid. The state of Circuit 109 is also usually displayed as a lamp on the modem.

The full-duplex circuit has now been established and may be used at will. Serial data are sent to the modem on Circuit 103 and received on 104. Any temporary interruption of signals will cause 109 to become False at the receiver. In many systems, if 109 of the computer is False for longer than a certain time, the control software will disconnect the circuit by setting 105 and 109 to False. A similar automatic procedure may apply in the terminal. Normal shutdown, however, will follow a logging-off procedure between user and computer, and either the operation of a button by the operator or simply the replacement of the telephone handset will release the circuit. At the computer the effect is failure of 109 but in this case the computer is expecting it. Alternatively, the computer itself can release the circuit using 105 and 108, following the log off.

It has been emphasized that the FSK technique uses ordinary audio frequencies, without complicated modulations. Rather than generate the tones electrically onto the telephone wire, it is possible to generate and detect them in audio form in a device called an acoustic coupler (Fig. 2.18). This device transmits via the mouthpiece and receives via the earpiece of a telephone, mounted in a special fitting. The call is established with the telephone and then the handset is simply put in the acoustic coupler and transmission may begin. The acoustic coupler also offers a V24 interface to the DTE, so no modifications of the DTE are required. Its great advantage is that it is simple, cheap and can be used without interfering with PTT lines, or indeed informing the authority. For many years acoustic couplers were frowned on, but they became so widespread that they had to be accepted, and now CCITT issues a recommendation (V15) covering their use. Figure 2.19 illustrates a specification controlling the power spectrum that may be admitted from an acoustic coupler on UK telephone circuits. The acoustic coupler is, of course, viable only at low speeds using simple FSK modulation techniques.

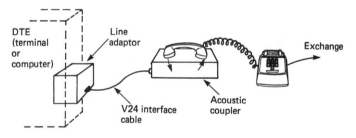

Fig. 2.18 An acoustic coupler

2.2.4 Local 20 mA connections and dummy modems for V24 connections

Many computer systems have locally as well as remotely attached terminals. Often these are connected by means of two current loop circuits, one for transmission and one for reception (Fig. 2.20). Typically the current in each loop is 20 mA and its presence indicates 'Mark' or 'Logical 1'. (Theoretically the reception of more than 9 space bits at a time, corresponding to Start and an 8-bit Null character, is impossible. However, this could occur if the loop broke, and

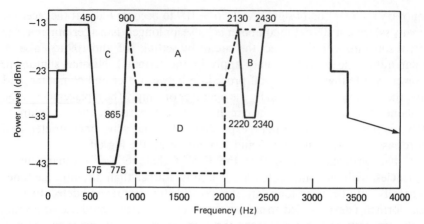

Fig. 2.19 Maximum permitted power levels. Signals (up to − 14 dBm) are only permitted in area B if accompanied by coincident signals in area A or if accompanied by coincident signals in area D at a power level not lower than 12 dB below the power level of signals in area B. The total power level of the combined signals must not exceed − 13 dBm. Signals are not permitted to occur in area C because false operation of trunk signalling equipment may result. The frequency range 400–450 Hz should be avoided if possible because a small percentage of switched telephone network connections have signalling equipments (500/20 ringers) that may be falsely operated by signals in this band

hence such a sequence of spaces is known as a Break character. It can usually be generated by a special key on a terminal's keyboard.) The line adaptors of the computer and the terminal with such an interface will be called '20 mA' or 'Current loop', as opposed to 'V24' or 'EIA' adaptors. Such line adaptors are 'active' if they generate the current. A 'passive' line adaptor merely switches or interrupts the current which is generated by its interlocutor. On each current loop one of the transmitter/receiver pair must obviously be active.

The 20 mA current loop connection is common, but frequently an installation will prefer to have all its line adaptors and terminals V24-compatible, whether remote or local, to simplify interchanges and reconnections. In this case a dummy modem will be used for the local terminals (Fig. 2.21). The dummy modem is simply a cross-connection box for circuits 103 (Transmit Data) and 104 (Receive Data). Often further cross- and back-wiring (as illustrated) is provided so

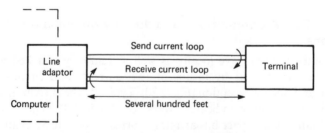

Fig. 2.20 Current loop interface

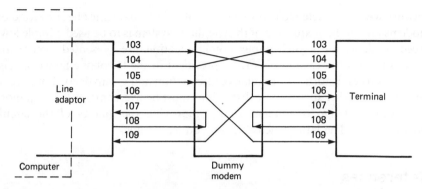

Fig. 2.21   A dummy modem

that standard software which may test circuits 106, 107 and 109 or drive 105 and 108 will operate without change. It is simple to manufacture your own dummy modem if necessary. Dummy modems are also implemented by cross-wiring in the cable between modem and terminal.

2.2.5 Other interfaces

As indicated previously the V24 interface is intended to be superseded by more modern specifications [1]. The limitations of V24 are essentially electrical. The voltages are not suitable for modern integrated circuits, and the common signalling earth is an obvious potential source of interference. The electrical specifications for the V24 interface are given in Recommendation V28. The effect of these problems is to limit the signalling rate possible on the V24 interface to a few tens of kHz, and the length of the circuits to a few tens of metres.

CCITT has recommended two improved interfacing specifications for DCEs such as modems. They are V10 (USA equivalent is EIA RS423-A) and V11 (RS422-A). (Additionally, in the USA the RS449 interface upgrades RS232-C to be compatible with later versions of V24.)

The V10 Recommendation covers unbalanced circuits (i.e. common signal earth), with logical $1 < -0.3$ V, logical $0 > +0.3$ V. It is compatible with V28 operated with voltages < 12 V. It can operate up to 100 000 bps; and at slower speeds over a distance of 1000 m.

The V11 Recommendation is based on balanced circuits (i.e. with individual return paths), and will operate at up to 50 million bps. V10 can be made compatible with V11 at slower speeds.

Finally it should be mentioned that the V10 and V11 interfaces use a 37-pin connector (defined by ISO 4902) supplemented with a 9-pin connector for a backward channel.

2.3 Summary

Remote serial transmission presupposes the existence of a medium. Many media are possible but the most widely used one is the telephone network. Since the network was constructed to carry voice signals, digital data must be converted by modems into audio frequencies if the telephone system is to be used. Simple low-speed modems for asynchronous communication are presented. There are various forms of noise and distortion prevalent in the telephone network. The most serious of distortions are relative attenuation and group delay. If we are to send data at higher speeds these distortions must be overcome, either by a more sophisticated design of modem, or by improving the quality of the circuit (conditioning). The latter is feasible only on leased lines.

References

1. *Eighth Plenary Assembly, Red Book, Fasc. VIII.1, Data Transmission over the Telephone Network*. The International Telecommunications Union, Place des Nations, Geneva, 1985.

   V21 300 bps Modems for the Public Switched Telephone Network
   V23 1200/600/75 bps Modems for the Public Switched Telephone Network
   V24 Interchange Circuits at Terminal/Modem Interface
   V15 Power levels for Acoustic Couplers
   V10 Characteristics of Unbalanced Circuits
   V11 Characteristics of Balanced Circuits
   V28 Characteristics of Unbalanced Circuits

2. *Eighth Plenary Assembly, Red Book, Fasc. VIII.3, Data Communication Networks: Interfaces.*

   X20   Interface between DTE and DCE for start-stop transmission on public data networks
   X21   Interface between DTE and DCE for synchronous operation on public data networks
   X20 bis V21-compatible interface between DTE and DCE
   X21 bis Use on public data networks of DTEs which are designed for interfacing to synchronous V-series modems.

3. ISO, International Standards Organization, CP 56, Geneva 20.

   ISO 2110 Interface Circuits on 25-pin Connector
   ISO 4902 Interface Circuits on 37-pin and 9-pin Connectors

Chapter 3 Synchronous block-mode transmission

3.1 The nature of synchronous transmission

Asynchronous transmission was discussed in Chapter 1. Its chief characteristic is that it handles strings of characters with arbitrary intervals between each character.

In synchronous or block-mode transmission, data are sent as a block of consecutive serial bits, typically up to 4000 bits long. Although the data may be composed of printable characters, they could just as well be pure binary bits, e.g. the contents of a portion of computer memory. There are no start and stop bits between characters, and redundant bits for error detection are typically attached to the end of the block, rather than added as a parity bit per character. Synchronous transmission is properly called isochronous transmission because of the steady bit-rate. The word 'synchronous' refers to the DCE/DTE interface which carries clocking signals to enable the DTE and DCE to operate in synchronism.

3.1.1 Synchronization of bits and octets

Synchronous transmission is used at higher speeds when the efficient exploitation of line capacity becomes important, and the overhead represented by stop and start bits is unacceptable. However, by dispensing with the stop and start bits we return to the timing problems: how do we identify the bits on reception? How do we identify the characters?

The answer to the first problem is straightforward: a clocking signal is transmitted with the data to mark or 'strobe' each bit (see Appendix). On the V24 interface the modem delivers the strobe signal on Circuit 115 'Receiver Signal Element Timing (DCE Source)'. A transmission from ON to OFF on 115 signifies the middle of the received bit on 104. This, of course, presupposes that the receiver of the modem itself knows where the bits are, and this information it gets by extracting the clock signals from the incoming data stream. In turn this presupposes a modulation technique quite different from FSK (which conveys no timing information if, for example, continuous Mark is sent).

The V24 interface allows two mutually exclusive possibilities for strobing the transmitted data into the modem from the line adaptor:

Circuit 113 'Transmitter Signal Element Timing (DTE Source)'
or
Circuit 114 'Transmitter Signal Element Timing (DCE Source)'

Transitions from ON to OFF on 113 allow the DTE to indicate to the DCE the centre of the bits on 103. Alternatively 114 may be taken from the DCE to gate out the bits from the DTE, the OFF to ON transmission on 114 starting the bits on 103.

Circuit 113 is particularly applicable to dummy modem or loopback connections where it is fed into another adaptor's 115 (or its own). Circuit 114, however, is important when network-wide synchronism is required, for example if a multiplexer (see Chapter 6) is used. Line adaptors for block-mode transmission, synchronous line adaptors, must support Circuit 115, and 113 and/or 114.

The second problem is: how do we identify the octets or characters? The procedure is to begin each block with a few special synchronization characters (e.g. SYN). The receiving DTE will shift the incoming bit-stream, bit by bit, looking each time at an 8-bit window, if there are 8 bits per character. The contents of the window will be compared with the SYN character, and if a match occurs synchronization has potentially been achieved. The DTE will then take the following, non-overlapping 8 bits and if these correspond to SYN, character synchronization is complete. If either of these tests fails, the receiver simply continues shifting the next bit in and searching for SYN as though it were starting again at the beginning. This synchronization of characters between sender and receiver can be done by software in the receiving computer, but is more commonly performed by special circuits in the synchronous line adaptor or its USART (Fig. 3.1). Once synchronization has been established, the receiving line adaptor accumulates 8 bits, then passes them to the computer; accumulates another 8 bits, etc. It will usually be double-buffered on input and output as in the case of the asynchronous line adaptor.

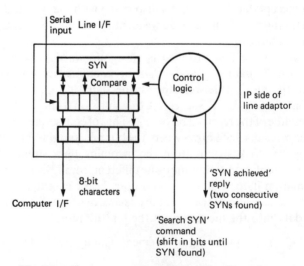

Fig. 3.1   Character synchronization in a line adaptor

3.1.2 The structure of a block

This section uses BSC (see Section 3.2) as an example. Other block structures, such as HDLC (see Section 4.2) are possible.

The computer is now receiving a stream of characters, which will initially be SYN characters, although some synchronous line adaptors can be made to 'strip', i.e. not pass to the program, received SYNs. The receiving software must then be able to determine when the block starts. One approach could be to assume that the first non-SYN character received, after synchronization, represents the start of the block. However, if bits are corrupted on the channel, as they will be, this could easily lead to an erroneous detection. Instead, it is usual to use a special character to indicate the start-of-block. We shall refer to this character as STX, Start of Text. The receiving software will consider all characters following STX as belonging to the block until the end-of-block is reached. Two methods can be used to determine the end-of-block: either a special character signifies the end (Fig. 3.2), or a count of the number of characters in the block (in some suitable format) follows the initial STX (Fig. 3.3). The end-of-block is usually associated with two characters, making 16 bits, for the detection of errors.

Fig. 3.2   A synchronous block with end-of-block character

Fig. 3.3   A synchronous block with a character count

The above scheme for identifying an incoming block on a synchronous line is typical of character-oriented line procedures. A line procedure is a set of rules defining the formats for transmission (e.g. the structure of the block) and the procedures to be followed when starting, pursuing and ending an exchange of data on a link. The procedure illustrated was 'character-oriented' because it assumed that the data were 8-bit characters (so that character synchronization was necessary) and that special characters existed, e.g. SYN, STX. Bit-oriented line procedures do not require character synchronization, but the receiver still needs to know where the block begins and ends. If the start-of-block can be identified, subsequent bits can be counted off, eight at a time, enabling character handling to be achieved if required; but, in principle, using a bit-oriented procedure, the block could contain data organized in any form.

It will be clear that synchronous transmission, unlike asynchronous transmission, requires a suitable line procedure if only to define the beginning and end of blocks. Line procedures may be, and are, applied to asynchronous transmission, but it is perfectly possible to send start-stop characters between two DTEs with no such conventions defining messages, error checking, etc. Interpretation of the data stream can be left to the human eye at a terminal. In synchronous transmission this is not so, since the continuous bit-stream received is ambiguous unless conventions for character synchronization and identification of the blocks (as opposed to interblock 'time-fill') apply. Synchronous line procedures are discussed later. Meanwhile we return to our first problem, bit synchronization, and the modems used for synchronous transmission.

3.1.3 Synchronous modems – the V26 modem

By 'synchronous modems' we mean modems that require a regular clocking signal at the bit-rate, or possibly some multiple of it. They are used for block-mode transmission, which, as we have seen, is used at medium and higher bit-rates, e.g. 2400 bps and above. The FSK technique for modulation, discussed previously, can be regarded as a form of amplitude modulation, in which a carrier, e.g. 980 Hz, is switched on and off at frequencies up to half the bit-rate, B. This requires a bandwidth of at least B Hz for successful transmission. Thus it is clear that simple amplitude modulation will not work within the effective 3000 Hz bandwidth of a telephone circuit at high bit-rates, and more elaborate methods are required. It is beyond the scope of this book to analyse and produce spectra for the modulation techniques that will now be discussed, but it should be taken that they are indeed compatible with the restrictions in bandwidth to be found on telephone circuits.

As an illustration of a synchronous modem, we shall consider the familiar if slightly old-fashioned CCITT V26 Recommendation [1]. This recommendation outlines a 2400 bps modem for use on 4-wire leased lines, thus providing a full-duplex circuit. An 1800 Hz carrier is used which is modulated 1200 times per second. Each signal element contains 2 bits, so the bit-rate is 2400 while the modulation rate is 1200 signal elements per second, or 1200 baud. Clearly $1\frac{1}{2}$ cycles of the carrier fit into each signal element. Two alternatives, A and B, are allowed for the phase modulation employed (Fig. 3.4). Each pair of bits is indicated by a phase change with respect to the preceding pair. In alternative B there is always a phase change, even if continuous 0s or 1s are sent. In alternative

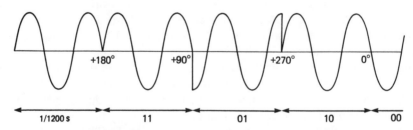

Fig. 3.4 Phase encoding (Method A) V26 modem

		Alternative A	Alternative B
Pairs of bits	00	0°	45°
	01	90°	135°
	11	180°	225°
	10	270°	315°

Fig. 3.5 Two methods of phase encoding, V26 modem

A there is no phase change, if continuous 0s are sent. Alternative A is illustrated in Fig. 3.5, but is now little used. The clock may be extracted at the receiver from the phase changes, or from the carrier, or from a combination of the two. In practice, the receiver timing, Circuit 115, is most likely to be driven by a local oscillator which is continuously adjusted by the incoming signal to maintain synchronism. The modem transmits continuous 1s when Circuit 106 is still OFF after 105 has been asserted.

V26 bis is a variant of V26 for 2-wire operation on the switched network in half-duplex operation. Alternative B modulation is used, with the possibility of operating at a lower rate under control of another V24 circuit, 111, Data Signalling Rate Selector (DTE Source). When this is OFF, the bit-rate is 1200, 0 being a phase change of $+90$, 1 being $+270$.

Both V26 and V26 bis allow for a simultaneous backward channel at speeds up to 75 bps using FSK modulation: Mark $= 390$ Hz, Space $= 450$ Hz. (Commercially available modems allow the backward channel to operate at up to twice this bit-rate.) In the case of V26, a backward channel exists in each direction, since the circuits are independent. In the case of V26 bis the single backward channel is in the reverse direction to the main forward channel. The backward channel is presented on the V24 interface as the circuits listed in Table 3.1.

Circuits 118, 119, 120, 121, 122 correspond to Circuits 103, 104, 105, 106, 109 for the main channel, respectively. Some computers have line adaptors which do not handle the backward channel as start-stop character traffic. Rather, they accept or deliver serial bits, corresponding precisely to Circuits 118, 119, from/to the computer, which is responsible not only for the generation and detection of the characters, but also for timing the bits. This is obviously unpleasant to program.

The purpose of a backward channel is to permit acknowledgements to be

Table 3.1 Backward channel interface (V24)

Circuit	Direction	Name
	DTE DCE	
118	$\longrightarrow$	Transmitted backward channel data
119	$\longleftarrow$	Received backward channel data
120	$\longrightarrow$	Transmit backward channel line signal
121	$\longleftarrow$	Backward channel ready
122	$\longleftarrow$	Backward channel received line signal detector

received from the far end without the need to turn the main channel around, analogous to the handshaking procedure with the timing circuits on the parallel bus discussed in Chapter 1. If data are sent from A to B, the acknowledgement from B to A of correct/incorrect reception could be as short as 10 or 20 bits, taking some 200 ms on the backward channel. This time is comparable with the turnaround times of the main channel, depending on the quality of the modem. Obviously, the ideal way to use the backward channel is to exploit its capability of operating simultaneously with the main forward channel. Here we require the concept of permitting further transmission of blocks while there are one or more still unacknowledged. For example, block N could be sent without waiting for the acknowledgement of block $(N - 1)$, which would travel simultaneously in the reverse direction. The backward channel is particularly useful on the switched network (V26 bis). On a leased line, the two high-speed channels, one in each direction, are normally all that is necessary unless two completely independent 2-wire circuits are effectively used.

The gap in the spectrum between the backward channel and the main forward channel (which uses from 1200 to 2400 Hz) corresponds approximately to gap C in Fig. 2.19. In many telephone networks this part of the spectrum is used for what is called in-band signalling, or carrying the signals which operate the selection mechanisms in the exchanges. Data, or voice, must not cause signals in this zone, otherwise malfunction of the exchange may occur, depending on its design.

3.1.4 More powerful synchronous modems

The V26 modem presented in Section 3.1.3 is simple to understand, but somewhat old-fashioned. A more recent phase-modulated modem is the V22 [1], which supports FDX 1200 bps communication on the switched network, using two carriers, one at 1200 Hz, one at 2400 Hz, modulated at 600 baud. This modem can operate in several modes. Essentially the analogue portion is always isochronous. Synchronous data are transmitted by ensuring (with the clock signals on the V24 interface) that they are delivered in digital form in strict synchronism with the analogue waveform. However, asynchronous digital data can also be handled, either by buffering characters in the modem and stripping

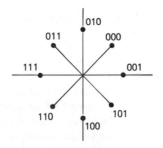

Fig. 3.6   Phase encoding on V27 modem

	Phase change
001	0°
000	45°
010	90°
Three 011	135°
bits 111	180°
110	225°
100	270°
101	315°

Fig. 3.7 Phase encoding on V27 modem

start and stop bits, or by simply sampling low-speed asynchronous data (300 bps) at the higher speed (1200 bps) and treating it transparently.

The technique of phase modulation is extended further in the case of the CCITT V27 modem. This operates again with a carrier of 1800 Hz but a modulation rate of 1600 baud. Three bits are phase-encoded per signal element enabling a bit rate of 4800 bps (Figs. 3.6 and 3.7). The bandwidth required is approximately 1600 Hz (1000–2600 Hz). This modem, and higher-speed ones such as the V29 9600 bps modem, employ a scrambler to 'randomize' the data. The purpose is three-fold: to ensure that the clock can be recovered at the receiver by forcing phase changes that might not occur if, for example, the sequence 001 were repeated for a long period; to ensure that the power spectrum on the circuit is reasonably 'flat' and without exaggerated peaks which might cause crosstalk, or upset the Automatic Gain Control of the remote receiver; to ensure that the adaptive equalizer (see below) at the remote receiver has a proper sample of the spectrum on which to operate.

The scrambling technique uses a feedback shift register (Fig. 3.8) which has the effect of dividing the bit-stream forming the data by the polynomial $G(x) = (1 + x^{-6} + x^{-7})$. For this purpose the bit-stream can be considered as a polynomial $A_n(x) = a_0 x^n + a_1 x^{n-1} + \cdots + a_{n-1} x + a_n$ where a_n ($= 0$ or 1) are the bits, a_0 being the first to be sent. The randomized output of the scrambler, $B_n(x) = A_n(x)/G(x)$, is sent to the modulator to perform the phase encoding. On reception and demodulation the original data are recovered by multiplying by $(1 + x^{-6} + x^{-7})$ in a similar descrambling circuit.

The theory of the scrambling process is complex and related to that for cyclic codes (see the discussion in Section 3.2). It is sufficient to say here that the circuit works by shifting a bit of data in at point A, where it is 'added' (addition is an exclusive OR, XOR) with the sum (XOR) of the last two bits of the shift register and then fed out at point B. Simultaneously the register shifts 1 bit right, and the

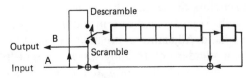

Fig. 3.8 V27 scrambler/descrambler (simplified)

output bit at B is also clocked into the first position of the register. It is a property of the configuration, which reflects the polynomial $1 + x^{-6} + x^{-7}$, that if the input at A is continuously zero then the output at B, generated entirely from the shift register, will produce a sequence of $2^7 - 1 = 127$ bits before it repeats itself. In other words the register itself will contain 127 different successive values, which is the maximum number possible, excluding all zeros, before repeating. Such a maximum length sequence is 'random' in the sense that its autocorrelation is minimum. In practice, the scrambling process is more complex than illustrated. The CTS Delay at the transmitting modem includes time to allow the remote modem's descrambler to synchronize with the transmitter's scrambler.

Three variants of the V27 modem (V27, V27 bis and V27 ter) are specified. V27 defines 4800 bps modem for leased lines of grade M1020 using a manual equalizer (see Section 3.1.5). V27 bis is similar but does not presuppose M1020 grade. An automatic adaptive equalizer is included, and 4-wire or 2-wire leased lines are allowed. Fall-back to 2400 bps working, using the scheme of V26 alternative A, is allowed under control of Circuit 111 on the V24 interface. V27 ter discusses a similar modem suitable for the switched network. In all three cases there is the option of a backward channel similar to that for the V26 modem.

3.1.5 Equalization

Higher-speed modems require equalizers, or the inclusion of additional circuitry in the modem to compensate for the attenuation and group delay characteristics of typical telephone circuits. This compensation is called 'equalization'. Figure 2.12a illustrates equalization applied to the attenuation curve, with the limits of the used portion of the bandwidth being amplified to produce a broader flat characteristic. Figure 2.12b illustrates equalization of group delay, the central portion of the bandwidth being artificially delayed with a similar objective. As the bit-rate increases from 2400 to 4800 to 9600 bps, so the required bandwidth rises from 1200–2400 to 1000–2600 to 500–2900 Hz, and consequently the need for flat attenuation and delay characteristics increases. For example, even the maximum C4-conditioning in the USA only guarantees relative delays less than 0.3 ms in the range 500–3000 Hz. This corresponds to half a symbol (signalling element) at 1600 baud and to some 0.7 symbols at 2400 baud, which is the modulation rate for the V29 9600 bps modem. Equalization in the modems is essential to improve these characteristics further.

Equalization can be performed in many ways. It can take the form of pre-compensation in the transmitter, but more usually post-compensation in the receiver is used. At speeds less than or equal to 3600 bps *statistical* or *fixed equalizers* are used. These perform compensation for the average characteristics of typical telephone circuits. Sometimes two or three types of compensation may be selected by a switch. *Manual equalizers*, in conjunction with some measuring device, are set up by hand. Adjustments are made to the circuits performing the compensation until a standard or training waveform sent from the far end is received with acceptably small distortion at the receiver's demodulator. The measuring device can be a screen on which the waveforms, the so-called 'eye-patterns', are displayed. A manual equalizer may achieve an excellent degree of compensation, but is obviously not proof against changing line characteristics.

Automatic equalization uses essentially the same technique as manual equalization, but the sending of the training pattern is initiated by the assertion of Request To Send, Circuit 105, on the V24 interface; and the adjustments are made automatically at the remote receiver, which knows what it is looking for. Indeed, the decisions required to make the adjustments obviously invite digital or programmed implementation, and most modems incorporate microprocessors for this and other tasks. The remote transmitter allows a certain time for this equalization to take place, before asserting CTS (106). Typically a longer time is allowed for first setting up the line, following assertion of 107, and shorter times for subsequent line turnarounds, as applicable on 2-wire connections. In the case of the V27 ter modem, 1074 symbol intervals, or 671 ms at 1600 baud, and 58 symbol intervals, or 36 ms, are allowed respectively. The total CTS turnaround delay on the V27 ter modem, allowing for carrier detection, equalization and scrambler synchronization is 50 ms. A further 200-odd ms may be added if protection against talker echo is required: this is achieved by transmitting carrier prior to equalization to cause the echo suppressor(s) in the circuit to operate.

An *automatic adaptive equalizer* not only adjusts itself to the current characteristics of the circuit by using a training pattern when the connection is set up or turned round; it adjusts itself using the received data. Perhaps this can best be illustrated by Fig. 3.9, which refers to the V27 modem. If distortion is not excessive, it is clear that the received symbols at point X really belong to point Y, the 45° phase shift corresponding to 000. Fine automatic adjustments can maintain all received symbols centred on their corresponding points in the phase diagram, provided that a representative sample is available – hence the desirability of scrambling the data.

The V29 modem for 4-wire leased lines, already mentioned, carries all these ideas a stage further. Phase and amplitude modulation are used (Fig. 3.10). Four bits per signal element are encoded, the first bit controlling the amplitude, the other three the phase (Fig. 3.11). The bit-rate is 9600 bps, the modulation rate 2400 baud, the bandwidth 500–2900 Hz, the carrier 1700 Hz. Fallback to 7200 bps with 3 bits per symbol, or 4800 with 2 bits per symbol, is possible. The scrambler polynomial is $1 + x^{-18} + x^{-23}$. The recommended CTS delay is

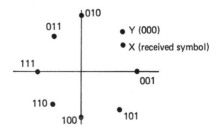

Fig. 3.9   Associating a received symbol X
with transmitted symbol Y

Phase	0°	45°	90°	135°	180°	225°	270°	315°
$\sqrt{2}$		0000		0011		0110		0101
3	0001		0010		0111		0100	
$3\sqrt{2}$		1000		1011		1110		1101
5	1001		1010		1111		1100	

(left axis label: Amplitude)

Fig. 3.10   Phase and amplitude encoding, V29 modem

253 ms, but, using a 4-wire circuit, this applies only on start-up or on recovery from error.

The method of modulation by phase shift, or by phase shift and amplitude, discussed above, is often known as Quadrature Amplitude Modulation (QAM), since it can also be achieved by amplitude modulation of an orthogonal (i.e. in quadrature) pair of sine and cosine carriers, which are then summed. The orthogonality facilitates demodulation since each component can be easily separated. The amplitude modulation is at the baud rate, and the carrier is at the centre of the spectrum with two sidebands. Other types of modulation techniques can be, and are, used – for example, Vestigial Side Band (VSB) amplitude modulation – but QAM is the CCI $\imath$ T-favoured technique, although not usual in the USA.

Finally, mention should be made of modems for wide-band circuits, for example on 60–108 kHz telephone group band circuits. Recommendations V35, V36 and V37 discuss such modems. V35 operates at 48 kbps. V36 is for 48 kbps to 72 kbps use, and employs the V10 and V11 electrical characteristics on the V24 interface. V37 is for 72 kbps to 168 kbps. These high-capacity links are typically used as trunk sections linking the nodes of packet-switched data networks.

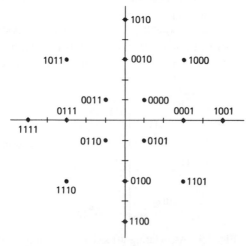

Fig. 3.11   Phase and amplified encoding, V29 modem

3.1.6 CCITT and other features of high-speed modems

The remarks on modems in the preceding section have concentrated on their basic features and on CCITT-recommended techniques. In practice manufacturers of modems offer additional facilities, either as standard functions or as optional extras, which are not necessarily compatible with, or covered by, CCITT recommendations. The role of CCITT perhaps requires further clarification.

CCITT's basic function is that of recommending actions, procedures, standards, etc., that will ensure that international telecommunication is possible, and not handicapped by incompatibilities between countries, users or manufacturers. For example, the V24 interface allows manufacturers to design DTEs for a world market, thereby giving users a wide range of suppliers. Such V24-compatible DTEs can be connected to a DCE in any country. Again, a V26 modem in one country made by one manufacturer should be able to 'talk' to a V26 modem in another country made by another manufacturer, because the modulation technique is compatible with the characteristics of the intervening circuit, as defined by M1040 or M1020, and is the same for each modem. This admirable aim encounters two problems in the case of modems.

The first problem is technical and administrative. Manufacturers have developed, and continue to develop, techniques faster than CCITT can review and approve of them. 9600 bps modems, using different techniques of modulation, were available from several manufacturers long before CCITT issued Recommendation V29. When it did so, CCITT in fact selected a technique already developed by one manufacturer, obviously causing commercial difficulties for the others. A strong argument can be made in favour of non-interference by CCITT in modems for leased lines – as is the case for V29. It is not often that a user would install, or have installed for him by the PTTs, two modems from different manufacturers at each end of his leased circuit, so that compatibility with an abstract standard is unnecessary. All that is required is compatibility between the two modems, which will be assured if they come from the same manufacturer. The user may additionally get extra facilities that might be unavailable if he were to select modems from different manufacturers, or restricted to CCITT norms.

On the switched telephone network, standards are more important since, in principle, a user with a modem might dial and be connected to any other remote user with a different make of modem. Alternatively, he may dial and be connected to a PTT-supplied modem at a switch (node) which eventually connects him to a remote user, after a series of analogue stages with modem pairs, interconnected by digital switching stages forming a network. In this case a standard is again important, but more at the national than the international level. (It is unlikely that a user would make an international call merely to get onto a network; he would more probably dial his final destination directly.) Many users and manufacturers would argue that technical progress is hindered by CCITT's slow operation, and its attempt to produce universal rules.

The second problem is political. The PTTs, who furnish the principal CCITT delegates, in defining the modems (DCEs) to be used throughout the world,

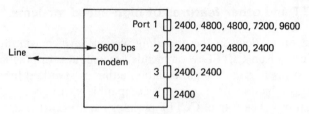

Fig. 3.12   Combinations of channel speeds on V29 modem

naturally begin to regard modems as falling within their territory of monopolistic supply. In many countries it is not permitted to attach your own modem to any telephone line – you must rent or purchase the modem from the supplier of the line, the PTT. Of course one is then restricted to the quality of modem available from the PTT, and to that PTT's delivery, testing, maintenance and other service facilities. In some countries it is permitted to attach 'PTT-approved' modems to leased lines, but it is very rare that modems on the switched network may be bought or rented from any other than the PTT itself. These PTT-approved modems must satisfy the authorities with regard to electrical safety by incorporating adequate fusing, etc., to protect PTT equipment and personnel. They must also comply with requirements as to the power spectrum emitted by the transmitter, to avoid causing crosstalk or other malfunctions. In practice PTT approval might be given only to modems complying with CCITT specifications, disabling the user from exploiting more modern techniques.

The following list serves as an indication of some of the more elaborate facilities available on higher-speed modems from various manufacturers.

Multiplexing: The various bits, e.g. four in the case of a 9600 bps modem, which make up a signal element need not all belong to the same data stream. For example, one might be from a 2400 bps source and three from a 7200 bps source. This merging of two or more data streams onto one circuit is called 'multiplexing'. Other combinations are clearly possible. High-speed modems may offer up to four such ports, each with its appropriate clock, CTS signal, etc., on the V24 interface (Fig. 3.12). The separate channels which are multiplexed into one high-speed channel must all be in strict synchronism. If the data sources are local to the high-speed modem circuit 114, Transmitter Signal Element Timing (DCE source) may be used to ensure this; but if there is a remote source, via a lower-speed channel and pair of modems, there are problems.

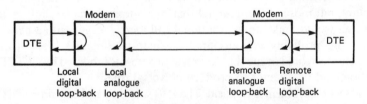

Fig. 3.13   Loopback testing with modems

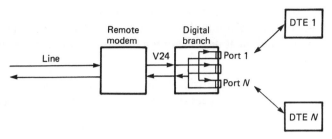

Fig. 3.14   Digital branching

Loopback facilities: To test modems and the intervening channels, loopback facilities (Fig. 3.13) are often available. These permit the outgoing data stream to be turned back as incoming at the local digital, local analogue, remote analogue or remote digital interfaces. Some modems enable this to be done remotely; so that an unattended remote modem may be commanded by a local modem to loop itself back.

4-wire and 2-wire working: Modems often offer a wide range of facilities for transferring from 4-wire leased line operation to the dial-up network if necessary, for example if the leased line fails. Such facilities include 4-wire to 2-wire adaptors plus telephones for making the connection; dual-dial interfaces allowing two separate unidirectional send and receive paths to be established; automatic calling equipment including the series-200 V25 [1] interface to the DTE, on which the digits and control signals are presented; simultaneous or alternative voice channels; etc.

Sharing and switching equipment: It is often possible to share a port between various DTEs. This digital branching would typically be used with polled configurations (see Chapter 6) (Fig. 3.14). Analogue branching at the line side of the modem may also be available, which is suitable for the hub of a polled network (Fig. 3.15). Most modem manufacturers also supply switching equipment for rapidly cross-connecting line adaptors and modems when a network needs reconfiguration.

Automatic speed changes: Some modems can automatically adjust the bit-rate, in synchronism at both ends of the line. This is useful when a multiported modem has a port inactive, since it permits other ports to exploit the spare capacity. Again, on multidrop connections (see Glossary) it may be possible to increase the

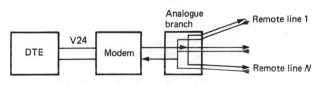

Fig. 3.15   Analogue branching

bit-rate, once equalization has been achieved at a slower speed. Automatic switching down of the speed may be desirable if the line quality deteriorates. Circuit 112 'Data Signalling Rate Selector (DCE)' can be used to advise the DTEs of these changes.

Fallback facilities: It may be possible to switch a modem on a leased line back to a dial-up line (either under local or remote control) in case of failure of the leased line.

3.1.7 Errors on data circuits

The previous section considered the nature of synchronous communications. However, it omitted one of the most fundamental aspects: whatever the techniques employed, blocks of data transmitted over a long distance circuit will always be subject to errors.

The errors that concern the user of a data circuit are those that result in the corruption of bits, causing the reception of garbled information. In the more serious cases bit or octet synchronism may be lost, necessitating reinitialization of the channel. Indeed, line quality may become so poor that transmission has to be suspended.

The bit error rate (BER) on typical circuits varies between 1 in 10^3 and 1 in 10^5. The BER is formally defined as the number of bits in error divided by the number of bits transmitted, so $10^{-3} \geqslant \text{BER} \geqslant 10^{-5}$ on normal connections. Diagrams like Fig. 3.16 may be obtained from measuring performance on a link. The diagram shows, on the y-axis, the percentage of all connections with a BER less than or equal to the corresponding value on the x-axis.

In the case of synchronous transmission, where data are sent in blocks, the procedure for recovery from a detected error consists in the receiver requesting retransmission of the corrupted block from the transmitter. (The use of error correction on reception (forward error correction) is discussed in Section 8.2.)

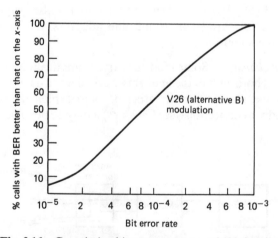

Fig. 3.16   Cumulative bit error rates on a 2400 bps line

This request is often called NAK (Negative Acknowledgement), as opposed to the ACK normally sent by the receiver to instruct the transmitter to proceed with the next block. The longer the block transmitted, the higher the probability of an error in it, and therefore the more likely that line capacity will be wasted with retransmissions. On the other hand, the shorter the block, the higher the proportion of non-data characters (e.g. SYN, STX) in the total data stream and the more frequent the incidence of pauses for ACKs or NAKs. Short blocks effectively reduce the capacity for data by giving a higher proportion of line capacity to the ACK, SYN and other overheads. There is obviously an optimum block length, between these two extremes, for a channel with a given BER and using a given line procedure (Fig. 3.17). In practice this usually works out at around 2000 bits, but block lengths up to 4000 bits, and even longer, are used.

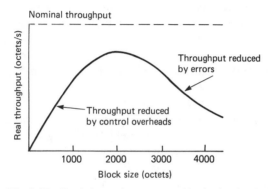

Fig. 3.17   Real throughput versus block size (typical)

The BER on a 2-wire dial-up connection can be 10 times greater than that on a similar 4-wire leased line. Much of the blame for this can be attributed to impulsive noise in the exchanges. Such noise occurs in bursts, a burst being generally longer than the duration of a single bit. Thus bit errors in the data stream are often not randomly distributed, but occur in bursts lasting a few bit-times. The procedures for detecting errors must be geared to this; and cyclic codes, or rather shortened cyclic codes, are used since they have particular properties suitable for burst error detection.

Some of the possible causes of error have been outlined already (Chapter 2). In general, although the source of error is almost always to be found in the quality of the circuit used, the modems are held responsible, since they profess to compensate for and be proof against the errors. The phase diagrams on high-speed modems can be used to analyse the types of error as already explained.

It is important to realize that it is the possibility of error on data circuits that gives rise to the need for line procedures and many aspects of the lower-level communications protocols. If data could be transmitted error-free from source to destination the protocols, which are the sets of rules governing the interchange of information, would only have to concern themselves with the meaning of the blocks transferred and what was to be done with them. In practice we need line procedures to ensure that blocks are transferred free of error, by correcting them, e.g. by retransmission, if errors are detected. We also need features in the protocols to ensure that blocks have not been totally lost, or put in a different sequence, error-free by the line procedure. In practice error-free communication is an ideal rather than a reality. The effectiveness of the error-correction procedures clearly depends on the effectiveness of error detection, and this is a function of block length. In typical cases the final BER, after error correction by the line procedure(s) on the link, is reduced to 10^{-8} or 10^{-9}; that is 1 bit in 10^8 or in 10^9 is in error.

3.2 Basic character-oriented line procedures

Most computer manufacturers have at one time or another developed their own synchronous line procedures, or line disciplines, for use between their computers and remote terminal devices. The original, and still most commonly used procedures, are character-oriented and half-duplex; the control of the use of the line is achieved by special characters added to the text stream being sent; and the positive or negative acknowledgements to the last block, or blocks, of data transmitted by the sender are not sent by the receiver until the sender has suspended transmission to await them. The International Standards Organization has issued a specification (Basic Mode) [2] defining such a procedure. It is very similar to the more well known Binary Synchronous Communications (BSC) of IBM [3]. The following description of BSC is not intended to be exhaustive, but rather aims to identify the characteristics of this type of line procedure.

3.2.1 Binary synchronous communications

BSC is half-duplex, or more correctly 'two-way alternate'. A block is sent from A to B and B acknowledges it. The block format follows the pattern discussed earlier. In the simplest case it starts with three or more SYNs, STX, the text, and an ETX or ETB character to mark the end of the block, and the two Block Check Characters (BCCs) for error-detection (Fig. 3.18). ETB signifies 'End of Block' whereas ETX means not only that, but also 'End of Text'; i.e. the complete message, which might have been broken up into blocks for transmission purposes, has ended. It is possible that a Header is attached to the block, in which case the block starts with SOH (Fig. 3.19). Headers are used to carry routing and

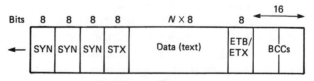

Fig. 3.18 A BSC block

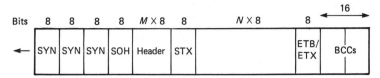

Bits	8	8	8	8	$M \times 8$	8	$N \times 8$	8	16
←	SYN	SYN	SYN	SOH	Header	STX		ETB/ETX	BCCs

Fig. 3.19   A BSC block with header

other information; for example, to identify which process or device within the destination equipment is to receive the block.

Once the sender has terminated a block with ETB or ETX he must await an acknowledgement from the far end. This can be ACK0 or ACK1 alternately, or NAK (Fig. 3.20) preceded by the appropriate SYN characters. Reception of ACK 0/1 allows the sender to proceed to the next block, provided that the sequence ACK0, ACK1, ACK0, ACK1 alternates correctly. If it does not, the sender assumes an error has occurred. Reception of NAK means that the sender must retransmit the last block. If the sender receives no acknowledgement within a certain time, because either his block or the acknowledgement was lost, he can request one by sending an ENQ character (with preceding SYNs), which should force the far end to send an ACK. The 0 or 1 will tell the sender whether his last block got there or not.

It is possible to send several blocks, separated by the ITB (Intermediate Termination of Block) character and the two BCC characters (Fig. 3.21) before awaiting an acknowledgement. This enables less frequent turnarounds to be achieved without reducing the probability of error detection. If any block is detected in error at the receiver, a NAK is sent and all the blocks must be

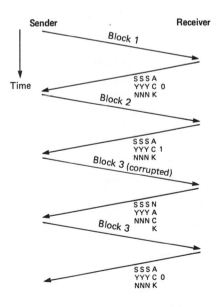

Fig. 3.20   Point-to-point BSC

| SYN | SYN | SYN | STX | Data | ITB | BCCs | STX | Data | ITB | BCCs | STX | Data | ETB | BCCs |

Fig. 3.21   Use of ITB in BSC

retransmitted. This technique is useful on lines with large turnaround times but low error rates.

A point-to-point conversation is initiated by the would-be sender transmitting ENQ to the receiver and receiving ACK in reply. He may then proceed. Conversations are terminated by an EOT sequence (Fig. 3.22) which may be sent by either station. An acknowledging EOT is not required.

Other facilities are available on point-to-point connections under BSC; for example, Wait-to-Acknowledge (WACK), which is an ACK but does not allow the sender to continue with more blocks. After a pause the sender should send an ENQ and proceed if he receives an ACK in reply; if he receives WACK he sends ENQ again (Fig. 3.23). Reverse Interrupt (RVI) allows a receiver to interrupt a sender. The sender empties his output buffers and then sends EOT (Fig. 3.24). The former receiver can now interrogate the former sender with an ENQ and proceed with transmission in the reverse direction once ACK 0 is received. The Temporary Text Delay (TTD) sequence, answered by NAK, is sent at 2 s intervals if the sender cannot send blocks for some reason such as a buffering problem (Fig. 3.25).

The above description of BSC on point-to-point connections outlines what blocks must be sent on a synchronous line, and under what conditions, if we wish to transfer data. The formatting of the blocks for transmission and the analysis of incoming blocks on reception are, of course, nearly always performed by software. Figure 3.26 is a very crude illustration of what is involved in both software and hardware at each end of the link. The sender must obtain or create the block and output it to the line adaptor and thence to modem and line, character by character. He must then 'scan' the input side of the line adaptor and accumulate the reply character by character. He analyses the reply. If all is well he loops back to obtain and send the next block, otherwise he must generate some other response (e.g. retransmission, ENQ, EOT). The receiver software scans the

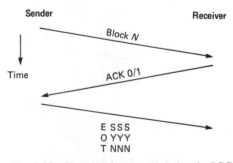

Fig. 3.22   Terminating transmission in BSC

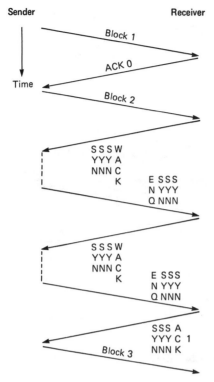

Fig. 3.23   Wait-Acknowledge procedure (BSC)

input side of its line adaptor. It accumulates a block, character by character. If it is acceptable, it stores or presents it somewhere; then it forms and sends ACK via the output side of the line adaptor, and loops to scan the input. If the block is not an acceptable text block it discards it, and sends NAK, or performs some other appropriate action (e.g. on receipt of ENQ). Such a software structure would be unacceptable on many systems as it implies dedicating a processor to the line, scanning for characters, etc. However, it is possible, because of the half-duplex nature of the protocol; and a computer system might have a microprocessor per line for this purpose. If simultaneous transmission and reception were permitted on the line such a simple program design would not work. In Chapter 5 the handling of communications links by software is considered in more detail.

Having seen a very primitive illustration of how BSC might be programmed and made to work in practice, we now turn to some problem areas. These are: timeouts and contention, throughput, error detection and transparency.

3.2.2 Timeouts

Timeouts are required to provide recovery whenever a response is awaited which may never come. If a block is transmitted and no ACK or NAK is received a timeout will reactivate the sending program to transmit an ENQ (see Section

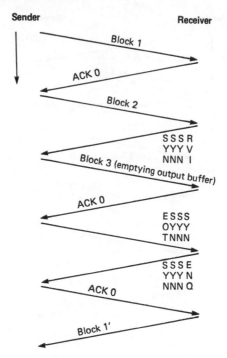

Fig. 3.24   Reverse Interrupt procedure (BSC)

3.2.1). There are other similar examples. The point is that certain actions, such as sending a block, are associated with the initiation of a timer to run for an indicated period. If a response is received before that period expires, the sender must cancel the timer. If the response does not come, the period will be timed out and the sender advised accordingly.

In the case of line procedures and protocols the timeout periods are usually long in computer terms – of the order of one or more seconds. This is because reasonable response times are often not really known, and a wide margin of error is allowed. But although the concept of a timeout is simple, and the precision required in real time is not very exacting, timeouts are often difficult to handle in the program implementing the procedure or protocol. This difficulty has various causes: the asynchronous nature of the timeout – it is a kind of interrupt; the fact that the timer is split between two logically different sections of the software, sending and receiving, with the sender being responsible for initiating the timer and responding to timeouts, and the receiver being responsible for cancelling it; the fact that some procedures require that several timers be running simultaneously, reflecting the existence of more than one outstanding unacknowledged action. In practice the facilities for handling timers provided by many operating systems are inadequate or inconvenient when applied to line disciplines and protocols.

A special case of timeouts occurs when two DTEs contend for a common line at the same time: e.g. if A sends an ENQ to B and awaits ACK0, but in fact

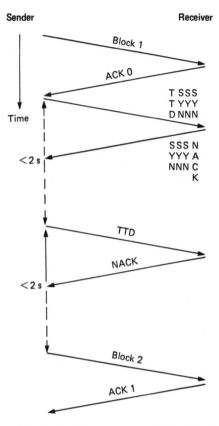

Fig. 3.25 Temporary text delay (BSC)

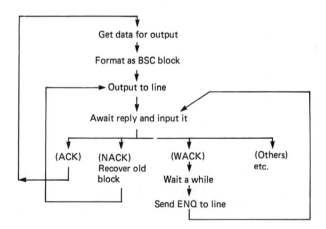

Fig. 3.26 Rudimentary program for BSC transmission

receives ENQ, B's bid for the right to send. The solution is to initiate separate timers at A and B, but of different durations. When the first timer expires, belonging to the DTE which was given higher priority, that DTE tries again. Thus, if A 'wins', B will receive an ENQ, reply ACK 0, and cancel its own timer. In the case of BSC 1 s and 3 s timers could be used for A and B, respectively.

This simple contention problem is an illustration of the more general problem that arises if many remote users contend for access to a single common resource. They could access a single point controlling access to that resource, the first arrival being served and the others being queued or rejected, but this strategy does not work if the resource is itself the means of access, for example a communication channel. A contender must seize the resource, find it has clashed with others, relinquish it, and try again after a timeout. Much time may be wasted, causing throughput to suffer.

Once again we have encountered a problem on long-distance circuits familiar on a computer bus – control of bus mastership, or bus arbitration.

3.2.3 Throughput

Throughput on communications links is measured in terms of useful information per second. Suppose we have a 2-wire 2400 bps connection between A and B (500 km apart): we should be able to transmit 80 8-bit characters ('card-image') in 267 ms, or $3\frac{3}{4}$ cards/s. However, if we actually try to do this using BSC we find that the throughput can drop to almost half of this.

Effective throughput, T_E, on a point-to-point BSC link is given by

$$T_E = \frac{\text{Number of useful bits sent}}{\text{Total time to send them}}$$

The total time taken to send the useful bits is the time taken to send them alone, plus the time taken to send associated control bits, plus the time lost in pure delays (D). Allowing for three SYNs, one STX, one ETB, two BCC extra characters on the transmitted block, and three SYNs, one ACK and one 0/1 on the reply, the total time spent in transmitting characters (D_C) is

$$D_C = \frac{8(N + 12)}{R} \times 1000 \text{ ms}$$

where N is the number of useful characters, and R is the nominal bit-rate of the link.

The delay D is given by

$$D = 2(D_{CTS} + 2D_M + D_P) + D_T + D_R$$

where

D_{CTS} = Clear to Send Delay. We have seen this can be zero, in the case of a 4-wire connection, or in excess of 1 s on the V27 ter modem. For the V26 bis modem a figure of 65–100 ms applies, although there exist commercially available 1200 bps modems, which are otherwise V26 bis compatible, offering CTS delays of 10 ms.

D_M = Internal Delay in the Modem. This could be due to scrambling, bit accumulation for sending several per signal element, etc. A typical figure is perhaps 2 ms.

D_P = Propagation Delay, which is about 7 μs/km. If PCM circuits, digital exchanges and, in particular, satellite links are used, this delay may be much longer. This is because such equipment employs buffering before forwarding data from one stage to the next.

D_T = The time it takes the Transmitting DTE to respond to an incoming block (e.g. ACK). This time is spent in interrupt handling and rescheduling the system, as well as actually processing the incoming block and preparing the next outgoing block. Up to 5 ms may be allocated to D_T.

D_R = The response time at the Receiving DTE. A similar delay to D_T could apply.

The factor 2, in the delay D, covers the reversal of the direction of transmission, so that D includes the delays associated with sending the block and receiving the reply.

Returning to our 2400 2-wire circuit, we may say

$$D = 2(65 + 2 \times 2 + 3.5) + 5 + 5 \text{ ms over } 500 \text{ km}$$

So

$$D = 155 \text{ ms}$$

$$D_C = \frac{8(80 + 12) \times 1000}{2400}$$

$$= 307 \text{ ms}$$

Therefore

$$T_E = \frac{8 \times 80 \times 1000}{D_C + D} \text{ bps}$$

$$= 1385 \text{ bps}$$

The 'efficiency' $= \dfrac{\text{Actual bit rate}}{\text{Nominal bit rate}} \times 100$

$$= \frac{1385}{2400} \times 100 = 58\%$$

If D_{CTS} is 10 ms, $T_E = 1818$ bps and the efficiency is 76%. If a 4-wire leased line is used with the carriers continually on, then $D_{CTS} = 0$, and $T_E = 1928$ bps and the efficiency is 80%.

The above calculations are indicative of what may be expected in the way of efficiency and effective throughput, using BSC, when no account is taken of the possibility of errors.

If errors do occur, major delays may result while timeouts operate, but in the most straightforward case of errors detected by the block-check characters, an extra delay $(D_C + D)$ will occur for retransmission and acknowledgement. If the probability of this occurring is p, and remembering that the retransmission itself may be corrupted, calling the total time for the block D_F, then

$$D_F = (D_C + D)(1 - p)(1 + 2p + 3p^2 + \cdots)$$

$$= (D_C + D)/(1 - p)$$

If the bit error rate is λ, and the number of bits in the block is m, assuming a Poisson distribution, $p = 1 - e^{-\lambda m}$. Thus

$$D_F = (D_C + D)e^{\lambda m}$$

$$= (D_C + D)(1 + \lambda m) \qquad \text{if } \lambda m \ll 1$$

In the case of our example we may take $m = 92 \times 8 = 736$. If $\lambda = 10^{-4}$, then T_E, the useful throughput, is reduced by 7%. If $\lambda = 5 \times 10^{-4}$, T_E is reduced by 31%. If $\lambda = 10^{-3}$, T_E is reduced by 53%.

3.2.4 Error detection

While 'horizontal' or 'vertical' parity checks (Fig. 3.27) may be used for error detection, particularly on asynchronous links, the cyclic redundancy check (CRC) procedure is by far the most common method for synchronous line procedures. The basic idea is as follows: the block to be transmitted is regarded as a polynomial $A_n(x)$, each bit representing a coefficient (1 or 0) of the next power of the free variable x. Thus

$$A_n(x) = a_n + a_{n-1}x + a_{n-2}x^2 + \cdots + a_0 x^n$$

where a_0 is the first bit transmitted. A remainder, $R_{n+1}(x)$ is calculated by dividing $x^k A_n(x)$ by the generating polynomial $G(x)$ of degree k. So

$$x^k A_n(x) = Q_n(x)G(x) + R_{n+1}(x)$$

where $Q_n(x)$ is the quotient, and the degree of $R_{n+1}(x)$ is less than k. In this arithmetic, addition is the exclusive OR operation, since the only values are 0 and 1. $1 + 1 = 0$, thus addition is the same as subtraction. We may write

$$T_n(x) = R_{n+1}(x) + x^k A_n(x) = Q_n(x)G(x)$$

where $T_n(x)$ is the polynomial sent by the transmitting station. It is composed of

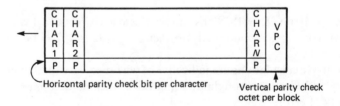

Fig. 3.27   Conventional parity checks

the data (shifted right k places), followed by the Remainder. $T_n(x)$ is clearly divisible by $G(x)$. At the receiving station, the same procedure is followed. The received block $x^k A'_n(x)$ is divided by $G(x)$ to produce a remainder $\bar{R}_{n+1}(x)$, which is compared with the received remainder $R'_{n+1}(x)$. $A'_n(x)$ and $R'_{n+1}(x)$ are not necessarily equal to $A_n(x)$ and $R_{n+1}(x)$ since transmission errors may have occurred.

If $\bar{R}_{n+1}(x) = R'_{n+1}(x)$ it is assumed that no error in transmission has occurred.

For an error to be undetected it must add terms to $T_n(x)$ which still let $\bar{R}_{n+1}(x) = R'_{n+1}(x)$. Let $E_n(x)$ be the polynomial representing the errors introduced.

$$E_n(x) = x^k E_{An}(x) + E_{Rn+1}(x)$$

where $A'_n(x) = A_n(x) + E_{An}(x)$, $R'_{n+1}(x) = R_{n+1}(x) + E_{Rn+1}(x)$.
An error is undetected if $\bar{R}_{n+1}(x) = R'_{n+1}(x)$, or

$$x^k A'_n(x) + Q'_n(x)G(x) = R_{n+1}(x) + E_{Rn+1}(x)$$

That is,

$$x^k A_n(x) + Q'_n(x)G(x) = R_{n+1}(x) + E_n(x)$$

or

$$T_n(x) + Q'_n(x)G(x) = E_n(x)$$

That is, $E_n(x)$ is divisible by $G(x)$ for an undetected error to occur.

In BSC, and also with bit-oriented line procedures, $k = 16$. In the case of BSC, $G(x) = x^{16} + x^{15} + x^2 + 1$. If $E_n(x) = x^j B(x)$, where $B(x)$ is of degree less than $k(16)$, then $E_n(x)$ cannot be divided by $G(x)$, since x is not a factor of $G(x)$. In other words, any burst error pattern of k or less bits will be detected by the procedure. Again, any error pattern of an odd number of bits will be detected, since no multiple of $G(x)$ – which has an even number of terms – can produce an $E_n(x)$ with an odd number of terms. More detailed analysis shows that $G(x)$ is capable of detecting other sorts of errors, but a substantial background of mathematics inappropriate to this book would be required.

The particular attraction of these shortened cyclic codes lies not only in the error detection and correction abilities, but also in their ease of implementation in electronic circuitry. Figure 3.28 illustrates how this is done. The feedback shift

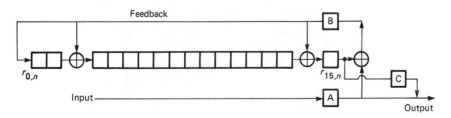

Fig. 3.28 Feedback shift register for division

register with gates A and B closed allows $A_n(x)$ to go out to line and the feedback process, which performs division, to operate. The feedback connections correspond to $\bar{G}(x) = G(x) + x^{16} = 1 + x^2 + x^{15}$. To demonstrate how division is performed consider what happens when one shift occurs. Suppose the register contains $R_n(x)$.

$$R_n(x) = r_{0,n} + r_{1,n}x + r_{2,n}x^2 + \cdots + r_{15,n}x^{15}$$

then

$$R_{n+1}(x) = xR_n(x) + r_{15,n}x^{16} + \bar{G}(x)(r_{15,n} + a_n)$$
$$= xR_n(x) + G(x)(r_{15,n} + a_n) + x^{16}a_n$$

If we multiply this equation on both sides by x^{M-n} and sum from $n = 0$ to M we get

$$\sum_{n=0}^{M} x^{M-n}R_{n+1}(x) = \sum_{n=0}^{M} x^{M-n+1}R_n(x) + Q_M(x)G(x) + x^{16}\sum_{n=0}^{M} x^{M-n}a_n$$

where

$$Q_M(x) = \sum_{n=0}^{M} x^{M-n}(r_{15,n} + a_n)$$

The terms in $R_n(x)$ cancel, leaving

$$R_{M+1}(x) = x^{M+1}R_0(x) + Q_M(x)G(x) + x^{16}A_M(x)$$

If $R_0(x)$, the initial value in the register, is zero, it is clear that the desired division process is performed. Thus the CRC characters for BSC can be calculated using this simple hardware, with the register initialized to zero. When the data are finished being processed, gates A and B are opened, gate C is closed and the remainder is shifted out attaching the 16 CRC bits to the end of the block. Figure 3.29 illustrates how the CRC characters are checked on reception. The circuit divides the received polynomial, $x^kA'_n(x)$, by $G(x)$, producing $\bar{R}_{n+1}(x)$ in the register. For the last 16 bits, $R'_{n+1}(x)$ is shifted into a separate register by gate B, and a comparison made.

Other forms of performing CRC calculations, including by software, are discussed in Chapter 4.

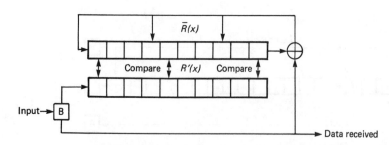

Fig. 3.29   Checking for errors on reception

3.2.5 Transparency

The most serious topic associated with character-oriented line procedures that remains to be discussed is that of transparency. A line procedure is said to provide transparent transmission to the user if it imposes no restrictions on the bit patterns sent by the user. The user's data are transparent, i.e. unseen, by the control software which looks for STX, ETX, ACK, etc. In normal circumstances if a user's data, which might be, for example, pure binary code from a computer's memory, happen to contain one of the special control characters of the procedure, then the receiving station will react incorrectly. For example, an ETB appearing by chance in the data would be taken to signify end-of-block when the block was not ended. If transmission is transparent, the user's data can contain all the special characters, provided the procedures for transparent transmission are observed.

In BSC, transparent transmission is achieved by beginning each transparent data block with DLE STX (instead of STX) and ending it with DLE ETB, DLE ETX, DLE ITB or DLE ENQ (abortion). DLE is the Data Link Escape character. Thus, unless the special characters ETB, etc., contained in the transparent data block are preceded by DLE they are treated as data, not as control characters. The only really special character is now DLE. Should the transparent data block contain a DLE by chance, the transmitting station adds another DLE to it so that the receiver will get a pair of DLEs. Whenever the receiver, while inputting a transparent block, encounters a pair of DLEs it rejects one as 'stuffed' by the transmitter, and passes the other through as data. If the receiver gets a single DLE, it looks at the next character, expecting it to be a control character, such as ETB (see Fig. 3.30). Note that this 'stuffing' and 'stripping' of DLEs within a data block applies only if the block is transparent, as defined above.

A special case remains. It may occur that SYN characters are inserted into ordinary data blocks in BSC, either to avoid loss of character synchronization when the transmitting station cannot keep up with the data rate, or because a SYN must be inserted at regular intervals with the character stream to reassure the receiving station that character synchronization has not been lost. Normally such inserted SYNs are discarded by the receiving station – perhaps by the hardware at the line adaptor itself. However, when transparent transmission is required it is possible that the data contain a SYN, which must not be discarded on reception. The rules for transparent transmission in BSC state that, if non-data

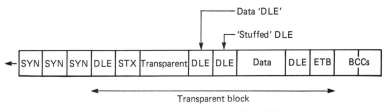

Fig. 3.30   Transparency in BSC

SYNs are to be inserted in transparent blocks, they must be inserted as DLE SYN, to be discarded on reception. A SYN on its own in the transparent block will be treated as part of the data.

Finally a word about coding. We have defined BSC in terms of characters, without saying how a character is encoded. In fact BSC is defined for three types of coding: 8-bit EBCDIC, 7-bit ASCII (usually with an 8th parity bit added) and 6-bit Transcode.

3.3 Summary

The way large blocks of isochronous data can be transferred between two remote computers is discussed. Suitable synchronous modems are required, to be able to use the physical link. A line procedure is then necessary to define the structure of the blocks and to specify how they should be handled on transmission and reception. A well known procedure, BSC, which provides the basic functions of error recovery and data transparency, is presented. It does, however, have limitations; in particular its half-duplex nature.

References

1. *Eighth Plenary Assembly, Red Book, Fasc. VIII.1.* CCITT.

   V26 2400 bps Modems for Synchronous Data
   V22 1200/600/300 bps Full Duplex Modems for the PSTN
   V27 4800 bps Modems for Synchronous Data
   V29 9600 bps Modems for Synchronous Data
   V35 48 000 bps Wideband Modems and Interface
   V36 48 000 to 7200 bps Wideband Modems
   V37 72 000 bps and Higher Speed Wideband Modems

2. International Standards Organization, ISO 1745, *Basic Mode Control Procedures for Data Communication Systems.* Also European Computer Manufacturers Association, ECMA-16.

3. *General Information – Binary Synchronous Communication.* IBM Order No. GA27-3004.

Chapter 4 Bit-oriented synchronous procedures

4.1 Scope and limitations of simple line procedures

The line procedure introduced in Chapter 3, BSC, addresses many of the problems of communicating between equipment discussed in Chapter 1 when reviewing an ordinary computer's bus. BSC supports the equivalent of timing circuits, because it is synchronous both at the bit and at the octet level. Provision is made for the control of mastership of the circuit by the contention procedure. Even a sort of interrupt is allowed with the RVI response. And of course all line procedures support error detection and recovery, which are not usually considered necessary on a computer bus, although timeouts are sometimes used there. Moreover, while we have yet to see the long distance equivalent of addressing, we have seen something similar to the bus control lines defining the nature of the transfer. Whilst BSC does not carry explicit information as to the number of octets in a block (as for example does DEC's DDCMP [1] procedure), that number is defined implicitly by the STX and ETB characters.

However BSC has various drawbacks which may be summarized as follows:

- It only handles data made up of octets (or at any rate of fixed size characters).
- It requires many special characters for control purposes, giving rise to transparency problems.
- It is half-duplex, question-and-answer, by nature, and is incapable of properly exploiting even an elementary full-duplex circuit, such as provided by the back-channel on a V26 modem.

These points are now discussed in more detail.

4.1.1 Variable-length bytes

Bytes are used to represent characters. (The word 'byte' is used here rather than 'octet' since the number of bits is not necessarily eight.) If the character set contains say 100 *symbols* then we need 7 bits (0 to 127) to be able to represent them all. However, it is very probable that some symbols occur more frequently than others. Could they not be given fewer bits, and rarer symbols more bits, thereby reducing the average number of bits per symbol and so saving on transmission capacity? If this can be done, obviously a different sort of line procedure is required to be able to carry 'bytes' of variable length. To discuss this possibility properly we need to look at *information theory* [2].

The information conveyed by the receipt of a symbol S_i is defined as

Information $(S_i) = \log_2 (1/p_i)$ Shannons

p_i = Probability of occurrence of S_i

(For the moment let us call the unit of information the 'Shannon' in honour of the theory's founder.) The above definition of information is chosen, because:

- If $p_i = 0$ (i.e. the occurrence of S_i is impossible) then the information conveyed by its occurrence is infinite.
- If $p_i = 1$ (i.e. the occurrence of S_i is certain) then the information conveyed is 0 Shannons.
- As p_i increases from 0 to 1, the information conveyed decreases, thereby agreeing with an intuitive idea of information.
- If two independent symbols S_i, S_k occur then the information conveyed is the sum of their individual information in Shannons.

This last point can be seen as follows:

p_{ik} $(S_i$ and $S_k) = p_i p_k$ if S_i and S_k are independent

Therefore

Information $(S_i$ and $S_k) = \log_2 (1/p_{ik})$

$$= \log_2 (1/p_i p_k)$$

$$= \log_2 (1/p_i) + \log_2 (1/p_k)$$

$$= \text{Information } (S_i) + \text{Information } (S_k)$$

Suppose there are eight symbols S_i ($i = 1$ to 8) of equal probability $p_i = 1/8$. Then the information conveyed by each symbol is 3 Shannons. Similarly, if there are two or four equally probable symbols the information conveyed per symbol is 1 or 2 Shannons respectively. In short the information conveyed is obviously closely related to the number of bits required to represent all the symbols (1 bit for 2 symbols, 2 for 4, 3 for 8, etc.). This leads to the idea: can the information content of a symbol, measured in Shannons, be used to determine how many bits should represent it? The answer is yes.

One method of using the information contents of symbols to determine their coding, developed by Shannon himself, is as follows:

1. Arrange the symbols in order of decreasing probability.
2. Calculate for each symbol S_i the number of bits needed to represent it, n_i, from $\log_2 (1/p_i) \leqslant n_i < 1 + \log_2 (1/p_i)$.
3. Calculate a function F_i for each S_i.

$$F_i = \sum_{j=0}^{i-1} p_j$$

Table 4.1 Shannon coding

	p_i	n_i	F_i	Symbol code
S_1	$\frac{1}{4}$	2	0.00000	00
S_2	$\frac{1}{4}$	2	0.01000	01
S_3	$\frac{1}{8}$	3	0.10000	100
S_4	$\frac{1}{8}$	3	0.10100	101
S_5	$\frac{3}{32}$	4	0.11000	1100
S_6	$\frac{1}{16}$	4	0.11011	1101
S_7	$\frac{1}{16}$	4	0.11101	1110
S_8	$\frac{1}{32}$	5	0.11111	11111

4. The coded representation of S_i is the first n_i bits (after the binary point) of F_i written as a binary fraction.

(It can be seen that these representations are unique, since $F_{i+1} = F_i + p_i$ and $\log_2 (1/p_i) \leqslant n_i$, or $p_i \geqslant 1/(2^{n_i})$, i.e. p_i alters at least the last binary digit of F_i.)

As an example consider eight symbols S_1 to S_8, with $p_1 = p_2 = \frac{1}{4}$, $p_3 = p_4 = \frac{1}{8}$, $p_5 = \frac{3}{32}$, $p_6 = p_7 = \frac{1}{16}$, $p_8 = \frac{1}{32}$, as shown in Table 4.1.

It will be observed that if we know the start of a symbol's code it is quite unambiguous as to when it ends (unlike what would happen if, for example, two different symbols were represented as 01 and 011). If we multiply the number of bits, n_i, for a symbol, by its probability, p_i, we obviously get the average number of bits per symbol used by this coding. The figure is 2.78; less than the three bits we might have used for each of the eight symbols.

Another, and more efficient, coding technique developed by Huffman works as follows:

1. Pick the two least probable symbols and allocate the more probable one a 1, the less probable a 0, and replace them by a new 'symbol node' with probability equal to the sum of their individual probabilities.

2. Repeat step 1, adding 1s and 0s to the pairs of least likely symbol nodes, and replacing each pair by a new node until only one node remains.

3. The 1s and 0s, read off in the reverse direction, give the code.

See Fig. 4.1, where the same set of symbols as in the previous example is used, and all probabilities are written in units of $\frac{1}{32}$.

It will be seen that the coding is still unambiguous (in the sense discussed above) and that the average number of bits per symbol is 2.75.

The question naturally arises: what is the best encoding that can be achieved? The answer is that a lower bound for the average number of bits per symbol attainable is the average number of Shannons per symbol, the *entropy*. In our example the entropy, H, is given by

$$H = \sum p_i \log_2 \frac{1}{p_i} = \frac{1}{32}(92 - 3 \log_2 3) = 2.73 \text{ Shannons}$$

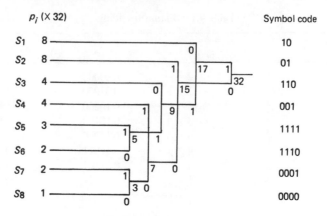

Fig. 4.1 Huffman coding

It can be easily shown that the maximum value for the entropy occurs when all probabilities are equal, and is (when rounded up to the nearest integer) the number of bits necessary to represent all possible symbols if no account is taken of their relative probabilities. The relationship between Shannons and bits representing symbols is thus very close, and information units, which we have called Shannons, are normally referred to as bits, and information and entropy are measured in bits.

It has been assumed that symbols are independent, which of course is frequently not so, since the occurrence of a particular symbol in a stream may make the next symbol certain, or others impossible (e.g. a U always follows a Q in English). The concept of entropy can be extended to such dependent sequences, and it can be shown that it still forms a lower bound for the average number of bits per symbol that can be achieved by any coding method. This, however, is beyond the scope of this book. The reader is referred to the references at the end of this chapter.

Our examples have not shown a dramatic reduction in bits per symbol; about 8%, or perhaps 160 bits in a 2000-bit block. However, savings could be more dramatic with a more skew probability distribution. Clearly a line procedure which does not require data blocks to contain an integral number of fixed-length characters is essential if this sort of compression is to be used. Clearly, also, the procedure must be very free from residual error, since once we have lost track of the boundaries between symbols that have variable lengths, it may take some time to find them again. Finally, for such compression to work, the probability of occurrence of the symbols used must be determined. This is not always easy. One practical example of compression is provided by the Group 3 Facsimile standard [3]. Here strings of black and white dots sampled by a scanner across a page are represented by special codewords designed to reduce the data to be transmitted.

Finally, techniques have been developed for encoding 'on the fly'; that is, building the compression table and performing compression in a single pass through the data.

4.1.2 Transparency again

With any line procedure that transmits blocks there must be a method of determining the beginning and end of the block on reception. If the beginning is known, the end could be determined by heading the block with a count of the characters in it, or of the bits if the procedure is bit-oriented. However, an indication of the start is still required, and this must necessarily be a special symbol – which can also serve to mark the end, thus making a count unnecessary.

The existence of a special symbol reintroduces the problem of transparency: how can it be arranged that such a special symbol never occurs in the data portion of the block, and yet permits any bit-pattern to be included there?

One solution to this problem is provided by the High-Level Data Link Control (HDLC) procedure. In HDLC, blocks called 'frames', begin and end with an 8-bit special symbol, the Flag, 01111110. (A single Flag may serve as end of one frame and start of the next.) To achieve transparency, within the frame, whenever five consecutive 1s are found in the data on transmission a 0 is inserted or 'stuffed' to ensure no false Flag is sent. On reception the following algorithm applies:

> If five consecutive 1s are encountered examine the sixth bit. If it is 0, discard it – it was 'stuffed' so 'strip' it. If it is 1 look at the seventh bit. If that is 0 a Flag has been found and the frame has ended. If the seventh bit is 1 an error has occurred, the portion of the frame so far received should be discarded, and a bit-by-bit search for the Flag starting the next frame should be instituted. (This procedure also allows the sender to abort a frame prematurely, if it wishes, by sending seven or more consecutive 1s.)

The above 'bit-stuffing' procedure is logically simple. It is obviously horrible to program, since computers work internally with fixed-length units (e.g. octets), and the insertion and removal of 0s involves elaborate shifting of bits from octet to octet. Bit-stuffing and bit-stripping are therefore performed by hardware, usually in the USART itself. The procedure also means that the length of a frame on the channel is uncertain. Assuming a random distribution of 1s and 0s in the data stream, the probability of five consecutive 1s is 2^{-5}, so an *average* expansion of frame length of 3% is to be expected. The *maximum* expansion is 20%. This has consequences for the design of a system if, for example, we are trying to fit frames into predetermined time slots as occurs in satellite systems.

It will be appreciated that if we are using a set of characters known not to contain the Flag, for example if we are sending pure text strings in ISO.7, then the gains achieved by recoding the characters in accordance with the compression mechanisms of the last section are likely to be offset by the expansion due to bit-stuffing.

4.1.3 Full-duplex communication

Full-duplex communication can be regarded as taking two possible forms:

- allowing return acknowledgements to occur simultaneously with further forward data blocks, thereby having more than one outstanding unacknowledged block as seen by the sender;

- allowing the simultaneous flow of data blocks in both directions.

HDLC provides for both forms at once. It may be asked: what users require a full-duplex flow of *data*? This question is not easily answered when considering simple bilateral conversations, without considering the nature of protocols at a higher level than that of the line procedure. However, if we allow that two or more independent bilateral conversations might be multiplexed and supported simultaneously on a single physical full-duplex circuit, it is clear that, being independent and uncoordinated, one conversation might require to send data in one direction while another wishes to send data in the other.

Considering only a single bilateral conversation which, we suppose, requires full-duplex data flow, various questions arise, such as:

- Can either interlocutor send data spontaneously, or must one wait to be instructed by the other?

- If spontaneous transmission is not allowed by both, is it permitted by one, who would be a sort of Primary Station to the other's Secondary?

- If the above options are allowed, how do we determine at the start of a conversation which option will be used; who is Primary, who is Secondary?

Any full-duplex line procedure should provide solutions to these and similar problems.

4.2 High-Level Data Link Control (HDLC)

HDLC[4] is an ISO (International Standards Organization) standard for a line procedure which aims to be applicable to a wide range of configurations and modes of communication. Not only does it address the kind of problems in bilateral communications mentioned at the end of the last section, but it also (like BSC) can be used in multipoint configurations (see Chapter 6). Various other protocols similar to HDLC exist, and indeed most of them are valid subsets of HDLC. Examples are IBM's Synchronous Data Link Control (SDLC) [5], and the Link Access Protocols (LAP, LAP-B) of CCITT's recommendation X25 [6] for interfacing to packet-switched data networks.

We do not discuss the full HDLC standard here, but only one variant, that used by LAP as employed on early packet-switched networks such as Euronet. (LAP-B is more commonly used nowadays.)

In this variant Asynchronous Response Mode (ARM) is used in which, once the link is set up, the stations at each end can send data spontaneously. Each station is supposed to contain two functions, a Primary and a Secondary function. The Primary function in one station sends commands to, and receives responses from the Secondary station in the other, and vice versa. 'Commands' include frames for setting up and clearing down the Primary–Secondary link, and data or 'Information' frames. 'Responses' include acknowledgements of various sorts. Effectively two simultaneous channels, Primary-to-Secondary, are set up in each

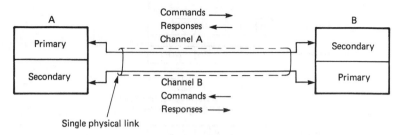

Fig. 4.2   HDLC – asynchronous response mode

direction, each channel carrying data in only one direction, both channels (call them A and B) being multiplexed on the one physical circuit (Fig. 4.2).

The HDLC frame structure is illustrated in Fig. 4.3. (There is much scope for confusion in the bit ordering. The least significant bit, bit 1, is usually illustrated on the *left* in the specifications, and transmission is from the left.) Enclosed between starting and ending Flags are up to four fields, all of which are susceptible to bit-stuffing. The four fields are:

1. *Address Field* (1 octet).   This is the 'channel' number. That is, it contains the Address A (= 11000000) when Station A's Primary function sends commands to or receives responses from Station B's Secondary function; and Address B (= 10000000) for Station B's Primary function commands to, and responses from A's Secondary function. (There is hardly a need for 8 bits here, but HDLC also handles more extensive multiplexing on multidrop lines.)

2. *Control Field* (1 octet).   There are three categories of frames, and the control field identifies them. The categores are Information (I-frames), Supervisory (S-frames) and Unnumbered (U-frames). Within the categories there is only one I-frame type, four (if SREJ is included) S-frames, and potentially a large number of U-frames of which we consider only four (see Fig. 4.4).

3. *Information Field* (*N* bits).   If present, this field contains an arbitrary number of data bits.

4. *Frame Check Sequence* (FCS – 16 bits).   This is a cyclic redundancy check using the generating polynomial $G(x) = x^{16} + x^{12} + x^5 + 1$. (See Section 3.2.4.)

Communication starts by asserting Request to Send on the local modem, waiting for Data Carrier Detect, and then transmitting the interframe 'time-fill' of continuous flags. When this has been achieved in both directions, either Primary

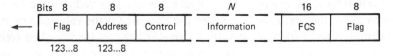

Fig. 4.3   HDLC – frame structure

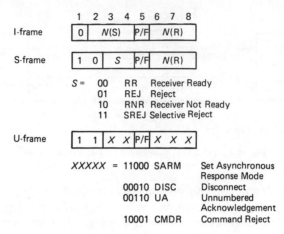

Fig. 4.4 HDLC – control octet. Note: bit 1 is the least significant bit

can, when it wishes, set up its 'channel' by sending an SARM Command (Set Asynchronous Response Mode) and awaiting a UA Response (Unnumbered Acknowledge). Timeouts are used to generate repeated SARMs if no UAs appear. Typically both stations will set up their channels more or less simultaneously, and when this has been done both can send I-frames at will.

I-frames have send numbers, $N(S)$ in the Control Field, running from 0 to 7 cyclicly, although an HDLC variant also supports modulo-128 as opposed to modulo-8 numbering (useful on links with long propagation delays, e.g. satellite). A station starts transmitting with $N(S) = 0$, then the next I-frame has $N(S) = 1$, etc. The $N(R)$ in the Control Field is used to acknowledge received I-frames. When a sender of I-frames *receives* an $N(R)$ it means that the remote station is positively acknowledging all I-frames with $N(S)$ up to and equal to $(N(R) - 1)$ (modulo-8) and is expecting the next $N(S)$ to be received to equal $N(R)$. It can be appreciated that a station should not send more than seven I-frames without receiving an acknowledgement, since beyond that figure the acknowledgement is ambiguous – did the receiver receive all sent I-frames or did it miss a whole cycle? $N(R)$s can be carried in I-frames in the reverse direction, or in S-frames. The RR S-frame in particular is used to carry positive acknowledgements in the absence of reverse data traffic. The procedure is illustrated in Fig. 4.5.

A station needs to keep three variables which we shall call X, Y, Z. X is the value for the next $N(S)$ it should send, incremented every time it sends an I-frame (except when retransmitting, see below). Y is the value of the next $N(S)$ it expects to receive, and is therefore also the value it gives $N(R)$, when it sends $N(R)$, all being well. If the next *received* $N(S) \neq Y$ an error has occurred. Y is incremented on reception of the next valid I-frame by the station. Z is the value of $N(S)$ in the last acknowledged I-frame it sent, therefore Z is one less than the last *received* $N(R)$. A station is not obliged to send consecutive $N(R)$s, but $N(R)$s may not 'go backwards'. A station should, on receiving an $N(R)$, check that $Z < N(R) \leqslant X$

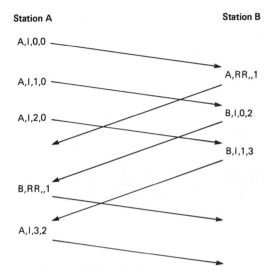

Fig. 4.5 HDLC – data exchange. Notation: Address,
Frame type, $N(S)$ if present, $N(R)$

(modulo-8), i.e. that the acknowledgement it receives acknowledges I-frames that
have been sent.

4.2.1 HDLC error handling

Errors are handled as follows:

- Any frame received with an FCS that fails the checking procedure is
discarded. This is because not only can its data not be believed, but also its
Control Field, and hence $N(S)$ and $N(R)$, are in doubt. As a consequence the
most common error is:

- An I-frame received out of sequence, i.e. whose $N(S) \neq Y$. The receiver sends a
REJ S-frame with $N(R)$ equal to the value of its variable Y. When the original
sender gets this it should then abort its current output if an I-frame (by
forcing seven or more consecutive 1s) and retransmit, in sequence, all
previously sent I-frames which had $N(S)$ values such that $Z < N(S) < X$ (see
Fig. 4.6).

- An I-frame that is received with an invalid $N(R)$, or indeed any invalid frame,
is responded to by a CMDR U-frame (now rechristened Frame Reject rather
than Command Reject). The original sender should re-initialize the link by
sending SARM, etc.

- If no response is received to sent I-frames, and the sender can send no more
(e.g. seven sent), after a suitable timeout it should re-send the last I-frame with
the P/F bit set meaning 'Poll'. The receiver should then reply at once with an
RR S-frame with the P/F bit also set in confirmation.

Other error conditions can obviously occur (e.g. wrong address octets), and

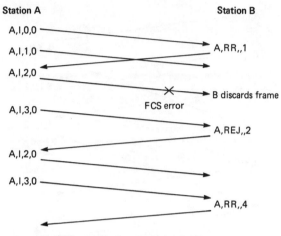

Fig. 4.6 HDLC – handling FCS errors

the use of the P/F (Poll/Final) bit is also more complex than indicated, but the basic scheme should be clear. (The P/F bit is used for polling in, for example, SDLC multidrop configurations.) A point to note is that in the absence of errors HDLC is very efficient, but when a typical FCS error occurs retransmission is demanded only on receipt of the next *correct* I-frame, implying a relatively long recovery time. Retransmission as demanded by the REJ S-frame is of *all* subsequent I-frames. HDLC defines an SREJ (Selective Reject) S-frame which on receipt requests retransmission of only *one* I-frame, as specified by $N(R)$. Subsequent correctly received I-frames need not be sent. The sender however does not know, yet, if they were correctly received, and has selectively to extract I-frames from its retransmission queue – the queue of sent but not acknowledged I-frames. In fact retransmission and the management of the retransmission queue is the bane of the programmer of HDLC.

Another S-frame, RNR, can be sent by a receiver if it becomes overloaded or short of buffers for incoming I-frames. The sender, on receipt of RNR (Receiver Not Ready) should send no more I-frames until a subsequent RR (Receiver Ready) is received. The use of RNR is questionable, since if it is to be effective it must be anticipatory, which is not always easy to arrange.

When a station finally wishes to disconnect the link it sends a DISC command, to which the response is UA. That 'channel' is then closed.

As an indication of other variants of HDLC it may be mentioned that there exists a Normal Response Mode (NRM), initiated by sending SNRM, in which the secondary sends only I-frames when polled (with the P/F bit) by the primary. Again LAP-B, as opposed to LAP, works in Balanced Mode, initiated with SABM, in which there is no primary/secondary distinction, and the link is set up with one SABM-UA Command-Response pair (initiated at either end), rather than an SARM-UA pair from both ends.

4.2.2 The Frame Check Sequence (FCS)

It has been stated that the HDLC FCS is a CRC remainder using the generating polynomial $G(x) = x^{16} + x^{12} + x^5 + 1$. In fact the procedure has other differences from that of BSC.

In BSC the end of block (ETB) comes *before* the CRC characters. Therefore, on reception, the calculation can stop at the end of block and compare the received CRC ($R'(x)$) with the calculated one ($\bar{R}(x)$). This cannot be done in HDLC, since the end of frame (because of bit-stuffing requirements) is *after* the FCS characters. An alternative, and equivalent, check on reception would be to divide the *entire* received frame, $T_n'(x)$, including $R_n'(x)$, by $G(x)$ and check for zero – but this requires a different circuit from what we have used so far. In fact HDLC uses another approach, as follows:

- Set $R_0(x)$, the initial value in the register, as $1 + x + x^2 + \cdots + x^{15}$, i.e. all 1s, instead of all 0s.
- On transmission calculate $R_{n+1}(x)$ as before, but transmit its *complement* $R_{n+1}^*(x)$ (inverting 0s and 1s) after $x^{16}A_n(x)$.
- On reception, initialize the register to all 1s as on transmission, then divide the *entire* bit-stream $T_n'(x)$, including $R_{n+1}'(x)$, by $G(x)$.
- Check that the result

$$\bar{R}_{n+1}(x) = x^{12} + x^{11} + x^{10} + x^8 + x^3 + x^2 + x + 1$$

or, in hexadecimal, 1D0F. (If we regard transmission starting with the left-most digit, the value is 1D0F as shown. On most computers data are output from the right (least significant bit first). In this case the value in computer memory would be F0B8.)

This curious result arises as follows (see also Section 3.2.4):

$$R_{n+1}(x) = x^{16}A_n(x) + Q_n(x)G(x) + x^{n+1}(1 + x + x^2 + \cdots + x^{15})$$

$$\bar{R}_{n+17}(x) = x^{16}(x^{16}A_n'(x) + R_{n+1}^{*'}(x)) + Q_{n+16}'(x)G(x)$$
$$+ x^{n+17}(1 + x + x^2 + \cdots + x^{15})$$

(It is $\bar{R}_{n+17}(x)$ because we shift in an extra 16 bits on reception.) If there are no errors $A_n'(x) = A_n(x)$ and $R_{n+1}^{*'}(x) = R_{n+1}^*(x)$. Also

$$R_{n+1}^*(x) = R_{n+1}(x) + (1 + x + x^2 + \cdots + x^{15})$$

so

$$\bar{R}_{n+17}(x) = x^{16}(Q_nG(x) + (1 + x + x^2 + \cdots + x^{15})$$
$$+ x^{n+1}(1 + x + x^2 + \cdots + x^{15})) + Q_{n+16}'(x)G(x)$$
$$+ x^{n+17}(1 + x + x^2 + \cdots + x^{15})$$
$$= G(x)(Q_{n+16}'(x) + x^{16}Q_n(x)) + x^{16}(1 + x + x^2 + \cdots + x^{15})$$

i.e. $\bar{R}_{x+17}(x)$, the remainder as calculated on reception, is the remainder obtained from dividing $x^{16}(1 + x + x^2 + \cdots + x^{15})$ by $G(x)$, which is $x^{12} + x^{11} + x^{10} + x^8 + x^3 + x^2 + x + 1$. If there are errors on transmission it can be shown easily, as before, that the same remainder occurs only if the error polynomial $E_n(x)$ is divisible by $G(x)$. As a result, this procedure has the same error detection properties as the normal one (with the same $G(x)$). The reason for choosing one $G(x)$ of degree 16 rather than another is because the valid *codewords* (i.e. complete frames including FCS) have a greater *distance* from each other. Distance is defined as the number of bits that would be required to be corrupted to convert one valid codeword into another.

If it is necessary, CRC remainders can be calculated by software. There are many methods [7], but perhaps the fastest uses table look-up. Speed is important since these calculations load a processor appreciably. The method supposes that the frame whose FCS is to be calculated contains an integral number of octets (!). It is as follows:

1. Assume we have processed so many octets, and have a current 16-bit remainder R. (In this algorithm, which it is supposed will be used in a normal computer, the least significant bit is on the *right* and is transmitted first. This corresponds to x^{15}.)

2. Take the next octet B (8 bits) from the data stream and XOR it with the eight least significant bits of R to produce $X = B + R_{8-15}$. This step is equivalent to shifting the register right eight times and XORing it with the data stream.

3. Pick off the least significant 4 bits of X and use them as an index (0 to 15) into Table LS (Table 4.2), consisting of 16 16-bit numbers to give $Y = X_{12-15}$th item of Table LS.

Table 4.2 Feedback shifting X_{12-15}	Table 4.3 Feedback shifting X_{8-11}
Table LS	*Table MS*
0000	0000
1189	1081
2312	2102
329B	3183
4624	4204
57AD	5285
6536	6306
74BF	7387
8C48	8408
9DC1	9489
AF5A	A50A
BFD3	B58B
CA6C	C60C
DBE5	D78D
E97E	E70E
F8F7	F78F

4. Pick off the most significant 4 bits of X and use them as an index (0 to 15) into Table MS (Table 4.3), consisting of 16 16-bit numbers to give $Z = X_{8-11}$th item of Table MS.
Tables LS and MS are the results of feedback-shifting the values of X_{12-15} and X_{8-11} respectively.

5. Construct W by XORing Y and Z; $W = Y + Z$.

6. Construct the new value of R by picking off the eight most significant bits and XORing them with W at the least significant end. $R' = W + R_{0-7}$ (shifted eight places right). This takes into account the right-shifting of R's most significant bits.

The Tables LS and MS are easily constructed. For LS and MS the first entry is zero. For LS the second entry is obtained from feeding back 0001 eight times, i.e. hexadecimal 1189; the third entry in this shifted left once, 2312; the fourth combines the second and third, 329B; etc. Table MS is similarly constructed by feeding back 0001000, giving a second entry of 1081, etc.

4.3 Summary

With HDLC we now have an efficient procedure for the full-duplex interchange of arbitrary strings of data between two communicants. Its transparency and error-detection mechanisms are normally implemented in hardware. The rest of the procedure must be implemented in software or firmware.

References

1. *Digital Data Communications Message Protocol.* Digital Equipment Corporation, Maynard, Massachusetts.

2. The fundamental concepts of information theory are due to Shannon, *Mathematical Theory of Communication.* C. E. Shannon, University of Illinois Press, 1963.

   Information Theory and Coding. Norman Abramson, McGraw-Hill, New York, 1963, is an excellent book on the topic.

   Digital and Analog Communication Systems. K. Sam Shanmugam, John Wiley, New York, 1979, contains useful material on this and related topics.

3. *Eighth Plenary Assembly, Red Book, Fasc. VII.3,* CCITT T4. Standardization of Group 3 Facsimile Apparatus for Document Transmission.

4. *High Level Data Link Control.* International Standards Organization. ISO 3309 HDLC – *Frame Structure.* ISO DIS 4335 HDLC – *Elements of Procedure.*

5. *IBM Synchronous Data Link Control – General Information.* IBM GA27-3093.

6. *CCITT Eighth Plenary Assembly, Red Book Fasc. VIII.3, Recommendation X25 Level 2.* International Telecommunications Union, Geneva, 1981.

7. 'On the computation of cyclic redundancy checks by program', P. L. Higginson and P. T. Kirstein, *Computer J.,* 1973, **16**(1).

Chapter 5 **Software for data communications**

In previous chapters the nature of serial transmission, asynchronous and synchronous with the associated line adaptors, has been considered; also, the need for modems when telephone circuits are used. Additionally, we have introduced some line procedures which determine how communication channels are used. In particular, these line procedures are responsible for error detection and recovery. Line adaptors and modems, however, are controlled by software or firmware. (Firmware is software implemented in ROM (Read Only Memory) or equivalent, so it is unalterable and appears like hardware. It is, however, a program in all other respects.) Line procedures (apart perhaps from bit-stuffing and CRC calculations) are entirely implemented in such software. How is this software constructed?

5.1 Handling terminals

Let us first consider a simple, probably familiar, requirement: the support of many terminals by a computer simultaneously, over a number of asynchronous full-duplex serial lines. This is the typical college or university configuration using scroll-mode terminals, which are terminals which act as though paper were used for output. (If a *screen* is used, when output reaches the bottom line of the screen, the contents are 'scrolled' upwards, the top line disappearing, and the next line appearing at the bottom.) The software supporting such terminals has, probably, the following functional responsibilities:

1. To accumulate characters, on interrupt, when input by the user at the keyboard, and to form a 'message' for passing to some other 'process' or 'task' for analysis. A 'message' is deemed to have arrived when either a maximum number of characters has been accumulated, or a terminating character, e.g. Carriage Return (CR) is read, or a timeout occurs due to the user's failure to enter more characters.

2. To output characters, under interrupt control, belonging to messages passed to it by some other process or task; to proceed with the next (queued) output message when the last was finished; and to suspend output when no more messages exist.

3. (Optionally) to echo input characters to be output back to the terminal, and

to ensure that echo does not start when message output is in progress; and, conversely, message output does not start when echo (i.e. input) is in progress.

4. (Optionally) to recognize special input characters and take appropriate action. Such characters range from control character sequences used to abort all current dialogue and return control to some master program (usually the one contacted when the user first 'logs in') to a simple Carriage Return which is echoed, perhaps, as Carriage Return followed by Line Feed.

5. To allow the terminal to operate in parallel, and unsynchronized with every other terminal on the system.

Such software would be called a 'Terminal Handler'. Its central character-istics are that: it supports many terminals simultaneously; as a consequence is interrupt driven; and is (as far as possible) *unintelligent*, leaving the analysis of messages to other tasks. (The control of a page-mode intelligent terminal is more complex than that of the simple terminal illustrated. In essence, for each terminal, a map of the current screen format is required, and specialized routines are needed for moving the cursor around the screen efficiently.)

Elaborating on these three topics it can be said that Terminal Handler software should be written in *re-entrant* code. Re-entrant code is code of which only *one* copy exists, but which can be used 'simultaneously' by many processes. This implies that each process, and there will be a Terminal Handler process per terminal, has its own *workspace*. Of course a single processor can run only one task or process at a time, but they will appear to be simultaneous if the processor changes rapidly from one to the other. Whenever it ceases handling one terminal the processor's controlling program records, in that terminal's workspace, all the current information, states of variables, etc., pertaining to that terminal, and when it returns to that terminal, it can pick up where it left off. The action of the controlling program in moving control from one terminal to the other is called *rescheduling* (the system). Re-entrant code is written in such a way that whenever the system is rescheduled a new workspace is used, i.e. selected in the rescheduling process, so that the code itself is unchanged, and only a single copy is required.

The system can be rescheduled for many reasons. For example it can be rescheduled by a clock, which effectively says, 'Enough of task A, let's run task B'. However, for our Terminal Handler the main causes of rescheduling are interrupts and completion. Whenever a new input character arrives from a terminal, the receiving line adaptor will interrupt the system to schedule the task which reads in characters from that terminal. Similarly, whenever a character has been output, an interrupt will cause a reschedule so that the relevant Terminal Handler task is activated to command the output of the next character. Once activated, the Terminal Handler will normally run to completion and then reschedule the system by request, since it has nothing more to do. On input, completion occurs when the character has been read in; checked for any special actions; echoed if necessary; accumulated into the message (i.e. put in an input buffer); and, when the message is complete, the message has been passed to some other task. Completion on output occurs when the character has been output; and, if the message has finished, a new message has been procured for subsequent output. It will be appreciated that interrupts are caused by external events, whose occurrence may or may not be anticipated, but whose precise moment of arrival is unknown. When an interrupt does occur it forcibly suspends the current program and makes the computer start executing code from some special location in the memory. In this location will be the *Interrupt Handler*, which 'fields' the interrupt and causes the Terminal Handler to be scheduled. It may not always be convenient to permit interrupts, in which case they are temporarily *inhibited*, at the risk of degrading response times. For example, we might inhibit interrupts when running our re-entrant Terminal Handler, since its bursts of activity will be very brief, and it would almost certainly simplify coding, without degrading response, to do so.

Finally we have said that the Terminal Handler should be unintelligent. Not everyone will agree with this. However, the moment intelligence is put into any device driver software, it becomes inflexible. It handles one type of transaction brilliantly but cannot handle another. Moreover it takes longer. For example, if our Terminal Handler were to *analyse* messages on input it would obviously take longer. If, while it is running on behalf of Terminal A, interrupts are inhibited, then Terminals B, C, etc., may suffer degraded response. If, on the other hand, interrupts are not inhibited, why put the analysis in the Handler rather than in some completely separate task handled decently by the scheduler? We do not labour the point.

Figure 5.1 attempts to summarize the software structure. An analysis task takes incoming messages (queued) from all the Terminal Handlers – which have only *one* piece of code between them, but each has its individual workspace. The analysis task queues messages for output to the Terminal Handlers. Each Handler is driven by interrupts (input or output) on one side, and by the arrival of 'buffers', when it has run out of them, on the other. The arrival of an output buffer, holding an output message, evidently requires an activation of the Handler. On input, the Handler needs *empty* buffers in which to accumulate

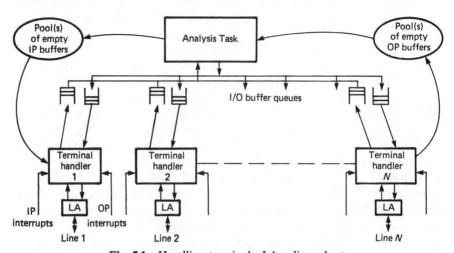

Fig. 5.1   Handling terminals. LA = line adaptor

messages. Maybe a shortage of empty buffers occurs, causing the Handler to be suspended; in which case it must be reactivated when a new empty buffer is available. The mechanisms for effecting these actions associated with message passing are discussed in Section 5.2.2.3.

5.2 A simple executive: TCBs

The previous example points to the need for certain facilities from the operating system of the computer. A computer's operating system is often very large, providing an extensive range of functions (such as file handling and support of system utilities), which will not be discussed here. We are concerned with the 'kernel' of the operating system, sometimes called the basic *executive*, whose essential function is to support multitasking, the control of many tasks running in parallel. We discuss such an executive [1].

Central to the multitasking executive is the notion of the Task Control Block (TCB). The TCB is the task, rather than the code which, as we have seen, can be shared. The TCB is where all information necessary to the executive to control the task is held, see Fig. 5.2. Held in the TCB are:

- The task's state, for example: Running (there can only be one TCB in this state if there is one processor); Ready-to-Run (awaiting a processor); Suspended (awaiting something else such as completion of input/output, or a buffer from another task); Dead (the task is dormant, perhaps awaiting manual activation).

- The contents of all the processor's volatile registers at the moment when the task last finished running. If the executive reloads all these the task will continue where it left off. Included are: The Programme Counter (PC); all general-purpose registers, accumulators, etc.; the Stack Pointer (SP) value for that task; the Processor Status Word (PSW) defining the state of the processor (e.g. priority) and other items such as 'conditions' (e.g. Carry, Minus) set by the last operation; any other relevant registers (e.g. Memory Management Registers (MMRs) defining the parts of memory to which the task has access).

- Timers peculiar to the task. The executive will very probably offer facilities

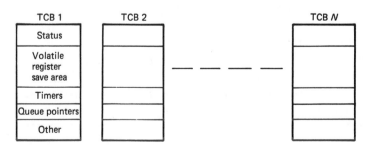

Fig. 5.2 Task control blocks

such as 'suspend the calling task for N ms'. The fact that the task is suspended awaiting a timer means that in the TCB either some timing count, to be counted down, is required, or some pointer to the external timer is being used.

- Queuing pointers. A task can be suspended awaiting a resource which it shares with other tasks, such as the processor itself, or an area of memory accessed serially by tasks. Tasks must be queued 'on' that resource, and such a queue is usually constructed by chains of pointers through the TCBs of the queued tasks.

- Other task-dependent information, depending on the design of the system. For example, each task might maintain a count of the number of times it has been activated; or the TCB could contain hand-coded initial values for volatile registers, so that when the task first starts up they need not be supplied from outside.

Besides having a TCB to itself, each task will obviously have associated code (maybe re-entrant code shared with other tasks) and workspace. The most typical workspace is the stack. In practice most processors have only one stackpointer so that each task will use this SP but with a different value, to point to that task's particular stack area. Additionally index registers or Memory Management Registers (MMRs) may point to a task's private workspace.

5.2.1 Scheduling

The executive controls tasks by means of their TCBs. Central to the multitasking role of the executive is the *scheduler* or *dispatcher* program, which decides which task to run next. The scheduler can be broken down into three parts:

- The scheduler itself, which makes the decision. When the scheduler runs no task is running, and the system is in a neutral state. If an external event occurs which might affect the decision process, it should be allowed to occur. That is one reason why the scheduler is usually made *interruptible*. An interruptible scheduler also permits the use of any sort of scheduling algorithm, from the simplest which picks the first 'ready-to-run' task in a list of tasks in a fixed priority order, to complicated ones which take into account a task's share to date of processor time, etc. (The point about not having code, especially long code, non-interruptible, is that the response of the system as a whole to interrupts cannot be better than the maximum time for which interrupts are inhibited anywhere in the system.)

- The *pre-scheduler*. This code must 'close down' the last running task; saving its 'context', i.e. volatile registers, in its TCB; changing its state, etc. The pre-scheduler must ensure that all critical information, such as the contents of the PC and SP are saved so that they can be later restored by a standard procedure (in the post-scheduler) irrespective of the precise cause which led to the suspension of the task and entry to the pre-scheduler originally. The pre-scheduler is usually 'delicate' code and therefore made uninterruptible.

- The *post-scheduler*. This code restores the registers, and reactivates the task selected by the scheduler. This is essentially done by reloading the processor's hardware registers from the selected TCB. Like the pre-scheduler, the post-scheduler is usually uninterruptible.

Changing tasks or rescheduling the system takes time, since the three above code modules must be run. Certain instructions in the processor's set may facilitate rescheduling, or 'context switching', but in most systems rescheduling will take 100 to 500 μs. This is wasted time, or operating-system overhead; and its importance increases as the number of tasks present and the frequency of rescheduling increase. For example, if a system is rescheduled 500 times per second, and rescheduling takes 200 μs, 10% of processor time is lost in this procedure.

When is the system rescheduled? Essentially, a task once running will continue to run until one of two things occurs:

- An interrupt causes the task to be temporarily halted. This interrupt could be from an input/output device requiring service; or from a clock whose purpose would be to cause a check to be made, to see if the system needs rescheduling.

- A call by the task on some routine providing a system service, which may result in an explicit or implicit suspension of the task. An explicit suspension would occur if the service called was, for example, to suspend the caller for 5 s. An implicit suspension would occur if the service was, for example, to provide access to more memory, but the memory was not available at that precise moment.

Whether the task is halted temporarily because of an interrupt, or because it entered a system service routine or Virtual Instruction (VI), one of two actions will result:

- Immediate return is made to the task from the Interrupt Handler or VI when the necessary work has been done.

- An immediate return is *not* made; instead the task is formally suspended and a new one run, i.e. the exit from the Interrupt Handler or the VI is to the pre-scheduler, scheduler and post-scheduler, not back to the task.

Figure 5.3 illustrates the flow of control through the system described so far. In the following sections we discuss some typical system services (VIs) and low level interrupt handling procedures, so that the executive may be 'completed'.

5.2.2 System services (VIs)

An executive may contain a very large number of VIs designed to provide all sorts of facilities to tasks. We shall discuss only a few basic ones, and those largely concerned with communication between tasks.

In a real-time system, in which the program as a whole is providing a function, tasks are not independent. We have seen how a device driver task such

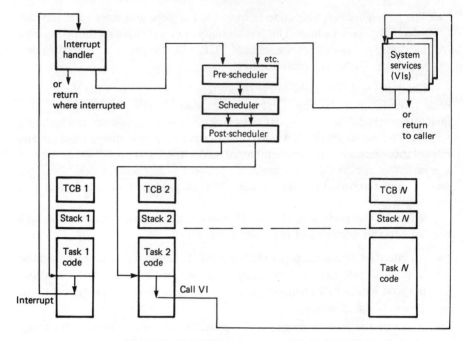

Fig. 5.3   Flow through executive and tasks

as a Terminal Handler might want to pass incoming messages to an analysing task, and conversely how a task generating messages will want to pass them to the Terminal Handler. This situation is typical. Not only will the 'application' tasks be distinct from the driver tasks, but there may be several application tasks; and even a single line may use several tasks to handle its line procedures and protocols. Later we shall discuss how and why functions are allocated to different tasks (to allow for queuing in case of temporary overload, to permit parallelism and to simplify design and coding); but for the moment we assume that distinct but related tasks will exist, and that they need to communicate with each other.

There are three basic methods of intertask communication which the VIs in the executive should support. These are:

- Use of common memory. Tasks A and B communicate by writing data in a common area to which both have access.

- Signalling. Task A communicates with B by signals carrying minimal information such as 'Stop' or 'Go'.

- Buffer passing. A buffer is a common memory area which, by convention and often by force (using MMRs), cannot be accessed by both tasks A and B at once. For example: A has the buffer, B cannot access it; A fills the buffer with data and passes it to B; B has the buffer and can read the data, while A can access it no more.

These three methods of intertask communication can be supported by some very simple VIs called *semaphore operations*. The notion of a semaphore is due to

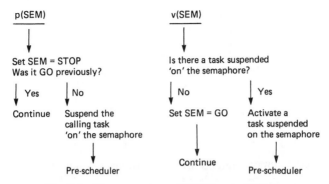

Fig. 5.4   The operations p(SEM) and v(SEM)

Dijkstra [2] who formalized the similar but *ad hoc* techniques used by earlier programmers. Dijkstra defined the semaphore as a STOP/GO Flag which could be tested by tasks. Two testing (and setting) operations are defined: p(SEM); v(SEM) where SEM identifies the semaphore in question. The operations are shown in Fig. 5.4.

These semaphore operations are designed to tackle the problem of 'mutual exclusion' when two or more tasks communicate via a common memory area. The problem is as follows: whereas it is always safe for two or more tasks to *read* from the shared memory area simultaneously it is not safe for some to read while another writes. This is because writing in the common area is almost certainly not *primitive*, i.e. it is not a single indivisible operation. On the contrary, changing the data in the common area probably takes several instructions, and if another task reads the data as the change is taking place, it may read inconsistent information. For example, suppose the common area contains several messages and a count of the messages present. When a new message is added the count must be increased. If the count is increased first, another task may come along and try to access the new message before it is present. If the count is increased after adding the message, another task may decide that the new message is not present (count not yet updated) and overwrite the new message with some message of its own. Many more elaborate (and simpler) examples exist. The problem of mutual exclusion is how to serialize access to a common resource to avoid an error, such as those of the example, occurring.

If there is only one *processor*, parallel access by different tasks to a common area can be stopped by simply banning rescheduling while a task is running the code which accesses the critical area. There are three objections to this:

● It is not *specific*. Why should rescheduling be banned because other tasks, some of which perhaps never access the common area, might access it at this precise moment? It would be much better to catch only those tasks that actually try to access it when access is forbidden.

● It is difficult to implement. In particular a major source of rescheduling is interrupts. What is to be done when an interrupt that requires a reschedule occurs but none is allowed? Interrupts could also be banned, with

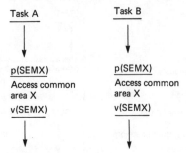

Fig. 5.5 Semaphore operations involving two tasks, A and B (mutual exclusion)

rescheduling, but this is even more drastic and could seriously affect real-time performance.

- It is often undesirable. The very task which has temporary exclusive access to the common area may cause a reschedule, explicitly or implicitly; for example, if it has booked the area so that it may load data into it from disk, and temporarily suspends itself while the disk transfer takes place.

Furthermore, if there is *more than one processor*, and communication systems are frequently built with multi-microprocessors sharing common memory, the notion of banning rescheduling (or worse, interrupts) temporarily becomes even more complex, since the various processors run more or less independently.

5.2.2.1 Communication via shared memory

The proper solution to communication via shared memory is to use semaphore operations on a mutual exclusion semaphore, whose initial value is GO. The system is illustrated for two tasks, A and B, but more could be involved (Fig. 5.5). Reference to the definition of the operations will show that only *one* task can access area X at a time. If a second, B, tries to access X while A is doing so it will be stopped by the p(SMEX) in B's path; and reactivated by A when A executes the v(SEMX) in A's path.

5.2.2.2 Signalling between tasks

Mutual exclusion supposes that the initial value of the semaphore is GO, to let the first task pass. The second method of intertask communication, signalling, is easily implemented with a semaphore whose initial value is STOP (Fig. 5.6).

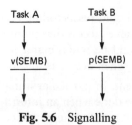

Fig. 5.6 Signalling

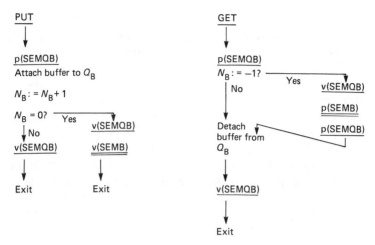

Fig. 5.7 Buffer passing

Task A signals B to proceed, B cannot go beyond the p(SEMB) point until A passes the v(SEMB) point. We have called the semaphore SEMB, because it is in a sense a *private semaphore* belonging to B, since B is the only task allowed to perform a p-operation on it, although many others might perform a v-operation.

5.2.2.3 Buffer passing

The third method of intertask communication, buffer passing, can be implemented by two routines which we shall call PUT(buffer) and GET(buffer). We suppose A PUTs a buffer to a queue of buffers from which B can GET it in due time. Q_B is B's queue and N_B the count of buffers in Q_B. When $N_B = 0$ there are no buffers in Q_B. We use the convention $N_B = -1$ to show that there are no buffers in Q_B *and* B is suspended as a result of an unsuccessful attempt to GET a buffer from Q_B. Additionally we introduce a mutual exclusion semaphore, SEMQB, to protect Q_B and N_B from simultaneous access by A and B; and a private semaphore, SEMB, for B to suspend itself when it GETs unsuccessfully.

Inspection of Fig. 5.7 will show that the order of the p- and v-operations in the GET routine is critical.

5.2.3 Implementation of the VIs

The semaphore mechanism is very powerful and, using it, many variants of the three basic intercommunication mechanisms can be built. Since the mechanism is so fundamental a few notes on its implementation are in order.

A semaphore is *itself* common data, so the p- and v-operations must be primitive, i.e. indivisible, so that A and B cannot perform 'simultaneous' operations on the one semaphore. This can be achieved with an adequate machine instruction set containing a primitive test-and-set operation. Alternatively, interrupts (and hence rescheduling) can be inhibited for the duration (very short) of the operation. This does not disaccord with the previous strictures against interrupt inhibition, as it is strictly local and very brief. In a multi-processor system the goal of primitivity, when two processors try to perform operations on the one semaphore at once, is harder to achieve. It really depends on primitivity at the memory access level.

Another point about semaphores is the suspension of tasks and their reactivation in the v-operation. A task suspended on a semaphore must be associated, when suspended, with that semaphore. Essentially a semaphore is not merely a STOP/GO Flag, but also a queue of the TCBs of the tasks suspended on it (see Fig. 5.8). The v-operation releases a task from the queue; which one? The obvious solution is to release the task at the head of the queue, but this pre-empts the decision-making proper to the scheduler. A better approach is to set the semaphore to GO; release all queued tasks; back-step them to the start of the p-operations where they were originally suspended; reactivate them all, and reschedule. They will now proceed according to the scheduler's priority mechanism.

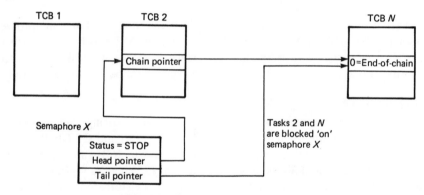

Fig. 5.8 Queuing on a semaphore

Finally, the PUT and GET routines can be implemented in many ways. Firstly, interrupt inhibition could be used instead of the p(SEMQB), and interrupt enabling instead of v(SEMQB). In certain circumstances no protection of the queue and its count is necessary; e.g. if the queue is a simple permanent circular structure where no attaching or detaching are necessary, and if the increment and decrement operations on the count are primitive. Additionally the whole scheme can be parameterized with the queue, semaphores and count in a table of standard layout, so that the PUT and GET use a single parameter to point at the table, another parameter serving to identify the buffer in question.

5.2.4 Interrupt handling

We have discussed some VIs (for intertask communication) which are illustrated on the right-hand side of Fig. 5.3. On the left-hand side is the Interrupt Handler – the other piece of code which may result in a system reschedule.

Each computer has a different hardware interrupt structure which the

Interrupt Handler must take into account, but certain functions are always present, as follows:

- An interrupt, when accepted by the processor, results in a forced jump to a specific location. The Interrupt Handler code starts at that location.

- Certain key items of the context of the task (or other code) running when the interrupt occurred are automatically saved by hardware, so that the interrupted program may be resumed later. These key items would include at least the PC. The items may be saved in fixed locations with the associated part being overwritten if a second interrupt occurs, or more commonly on a stack. Thus the interrupt is effectively a *forced entry to subroutine*.

- Individual sources of interrupt may be enabled or inhibited at will by software, so that if, at some moment, the program does not want to hear from a specific device it can simply inhibit its interrupt(s).

- A priority mechanism exists whereby some interrupts gain preference over others if they occur simultaneously; and also whereby the processor itself has a priority, which is dynamically under software control, and which causes it to ignore all interrupts of lower priorities. This priority mechanism may be very simple or very sophisticated.

- Interrupts that are temporarily ignored, because they are inhibited or passed over by the priority mechanism, are memorized in the hardware, and will assert themselves when enabled or priority conditions change. In short, interrupts are not lost.

On this foundation an Interrupt Handler must be built. Many types of Handlers can be, and have been written; but, again, they will usually have certain basic functions in common, as follows:

- The Interrupt Handler must be secure against the occurrence of subsequent interrupts when it is still running. This can be achieved by raising the processor priority above all potential interrupt priorities; or it can be done by using a stacking mechanism for repeated interrupts, which can be unstacked systematically later.

- The Handler must have registers wherewith to work. This may require explicit saving of more of the context of the interrupted program than that performed automatically by hardware.

- The Handler must identify the source of the interrupt. This can be done, in primitive processors, by interrogating all potential sources. Alternatively, vectoring (in which each interrupt causes a forced jump to a location specific to itself) may achieve the same end.

- The Handler must get rid of the interrupt so that the same interrupt does not immediately re-occur on completion of the Handler. This can be done by inhibiting it. More usually an appropriate input/output operation on the interrupting device will achieve the same result. For example, an interrupt states that a new input character from a serial line has been assembled by the line adaptor and is ready to be read. Reading the character from the line adaptor will remove the interrupt, by hardware.

- The Handler must interface to the Device Driver, which will usually be a task, or very like a task as we have defined it. This is a tricky area in which many approaches can be used. Essentially, if the Interrupt Handler does not perform input/output then it must schedule the Driver to do it (with the interrupt still inhibited). Alternatively, if it does perform input/output, then it must put the input data to or extract the output data from some area shared between it and the Driver.

5.2.4.1 A simple method of handling interrupts

A very simple interrupt handling approach is as follows: when an interrupt occurs the Handler automatically inhibits it, activates the Driver, and reschedules the system. The Driver task performs the associated input/output operation and, when it is ready for a new interrupt, calls a Wait-for-Interrupt (WFI) VI whose function is as shown in Fig. 5.9.

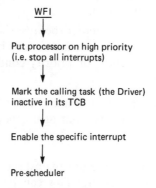

Fig. 5.9 Wait-for-Interrupt (WFI) VI

In due course interrupts, generally, will be allowed again, and a new interrupt from the device in question will cause the Driver to be restarted following the WFI call. A simple output driver, taking buffers of characters from a queue for output under interrupt control would then look like Fig. 5.10.

An input driver built on the same principles would look like Fig. 5.11.

Note that there are certain problems that are more acute with input than with output. For example: input is not always spontaneous (as from a keyboard), some devices needing prior activation by software; it is not always clear what is the 'last' character (Carriage Return? a count exhausted?), and there may be a need for a timeout mechanism to handle the case when a user simply stops typing in mid-line; the destination task for the full buffer is not always self-evident, it may depend on the contents of the buffer.

Note also that the Terminal Handler discussed earlier was more complex

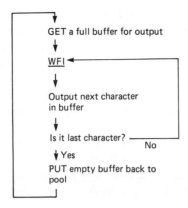

Fig. 5.10   A simple output driver

than these two drivers, since it handled both output and input in a co-ordinated fashion, and provided for the optional echoing of input characters.

The strategy for handling interrupts using the WFI VI discussed above has a major disadvantage, viz.: the system is rescheduled on every interrupt, implying a large overhead. If a Direct Memory Access (DMA) device is in use interrupts will occur on completion of block transfers, rather than on every character. Non-DMA devices can be handled by providing a simulated DMA facility in the software. For example, the WFI VI could be altered to provide a pointer to a block and a count of characters to the Interrupt Handler. The Interrupt Handler would output characters from the block as each interrupt occurred, without reactivating the Driver and rescheduling the system. The Interrupt Handler would return directly to the interrupted program on completion, and go to the pre-scheduler only when a whole block was output. This policy can be successfully carried a stage further: no rescheduling on device interrupts at all. Instead, a clock interrupt is used to reschedule the system say 20 times per second.

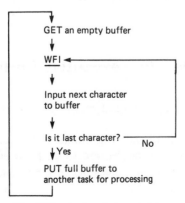

Fig. 5.11   A simple input driver

Such a policy supposes a certain degree of buffering between the Driver and the Interrupt Handler, to hold characters between reschedules. Very significant improvements in the performance of systems which are heavily input/output dependent (as are communication systems) can be achieved by judiciously controlling the frequency and complexity of rescheduling – particularly when a reschedule involves remapping the memory (changing MMRs).

In many commercial real-time executives [3] it is possible to write one's own Device Driver. In such systems there is usually no single centralized Interrupt Handler, but rather one per device, often directly entered by the vectoring mechanism mentioned earlier. The Interrupt Handler will thus appear in the Device Driver's code module, but logically it is as we have described it: a separate unit, interfacing to the Driver via a special mechanism.

5.2.5 Other VIs, timer control

Besides the semaphore operations, buffer-passing VIs and the WFI already described, many other VIs can exist or be invented. One important category is that concerned with time. For example:

- a VI to suspend a task for a given time, or until a specified hour is reached;
- a VI to cause a software interrupt at a certain time, without suspending the calling task. A software interrupt is one generated by software, e.g. the executive, and which often can occur when the task which it is supposed to activate is already active. This requires careful handling! An example could be an interrupt requesting retransmission of an HDLC I-frame to which no response has been received after the elapse of a certain time.

Additionally timeouts can be associated with input/output operations. For example, two continuations following the WFI call in a Driver's code could be provided: the normal one for when the interrupt occurs; an error one for when the interrupt does not occur after the elapse of a certain time. In all these cases there will be associated with the task, and thus probably in its TCB, one or more timing counts which are counted down by the executive in response to clock interrupts and result in a reschedule, software interrupt or similar event, when zero is reached.

5.3 Using the real-time executive for line procedure software

How is a multitasking executive used by the programmer of communications software? [4].

The first responsibility of the programmer is to design the *structure* of his code. How many tasks does he require to perform efficiently the functions required of it? What are the interfaces between those tasks (shared memory? signalling? buffers?); and what are the external interfaces to interrupt-driven communication lines and to the user's application software? In deciding how many tasks there will be, and in allocating functions to them, the following general rules apply:

- Two functions must be in separate tasks if they require to be run in parallel. For example, input/output from/to a line must proceed in parallel with obeying the protocol in HDLC; because one frame can follow immediately on another, and any line speeds resulting in aggregate character rates of more than 1000 characters per second (cps) will almost certainly leave too short a time between characters to perform a complete pass through the protocol module.

- Separate tasks are also required if buffering is to be provided between two functions. For example, an application may generate the equivalent of many data frames for transmission at a go. It will want to pass them all to the communications software at once, and let them be buffered there for subsequent serial output.

- If a system is likely to suffer sudden peak loads, with the consequent need to suspend less urgent functions in favour of critical ones, separate low priority and high priority tasks should be allocated to those functions.

- It is often a good idea to allocate distinct functions to distinct tasks simply to clarify the program, and to be able to give self-contained modules to programmers for implementation.

Thus there are various reasons for having many tasks. On the other hand, the more tasks, the more interfaces between them there are – and these interfaces must be rigorously defined, especially if different programmers tackle different tasks. In general, fewer tasks imply more complex but fewer interfaces; many tasks imply simpler but more interfaces. Many tasks also imply more rescheduling (overhead) and usually more buffering – and excessive buffering can waste memory and result in unacceptable delays.

As an example, consider programming an HDLC module for a synchronous line, with a software interface to an application. Since the procedure is full-duplex and 'continuous' (i.e. no pause for acknowledgements as in BSC) separate interrupt-driven input and output driver tasks are obviously indicated. The function of the input driver is to recognize and assemble incoming frames, to throw away those with FCS errors, and to pass good frames to the HDLC procedure task(s) for analysis and action. The function of the output driver is to take HDLC frames from the HDLC task(s) and ensure that the FCS is generated and appended. (Generally, FCS generation and checking, and of course bit-stuffing and stripping, is done by hardware, and the drivers directly control this hardware.) Secondary functions of the drivers, with the hardware, are to handle the abortion of frames, and to control the modem on the line.

There is clearly one, or more, HDLC task(s) independent of the application, because the HDLC procedure must continue at a high priority when the line is busy, even thogh the application itself is active. The question is: is there one HDLC task, or two (one for input, one for output)?

A single HDLC task is illustrated in Fig. 5.12. Its functions are:

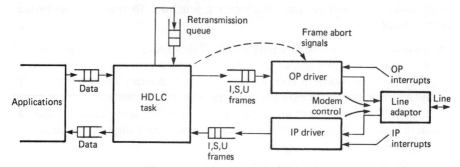

Fig. 5.12   HDLC as a single task

- to accept data buffers from the application and to build them into I-frames for passing to the output driver;
- to accept I-frames from the input driver and to put them into data buffers for passing to the application;
- to generate appropriate frames (RRs, etc.) for output to the line in response to received input I-frames;
- to generate commands for output to the line under certain circumstances such as no response timeouts;
- to maintain a retransmission queue, and to retransmit I-frames when requested (e.g. on receipt of REJ);
- to process incoming S- and U-frames and to update system variables as appropriate, and generate responses;
- to initialize and reinitialize the line as appropriate (send SARM or SABM).

The disadvantage of using a single HDLC task is its relative complexity. It can be activated by: incoming frames from the input driver; outgoing data buffers from the application; expiry of timeouts. It has three sources of full buffers: input queue from driver; output queue from application; retransmission queue. It requires pools of empty buffers for output S- and U-frames and probably for retransmission frames depending on the design. It is not easy to see how it could be built with only the simple GET (and wait if no buffer available) mechanism illustrated earlier, since perhaps nothing arrives on that queue, so the task is suspended and does not notice arrival on another queue. A more general signalling mechanism ('You-have-work-to-do') is required followed by an interrogation (without suspension) by the task of all possible sources. An additional complexity is the need for the task to be able to abort frames already queued for output to the driver, in case of a procedure error.

Figure 5.13 illustrates HDLC with two tasks, one for output, one for input. The system is simpler with regard to handling the interfaces to drivers and the application. Each task essentially looks only one way for work: to the application for output work; to the input driver for input work. But this is not completely true. The two tasks must communicate to pass, for example, $N(R)$ values. This

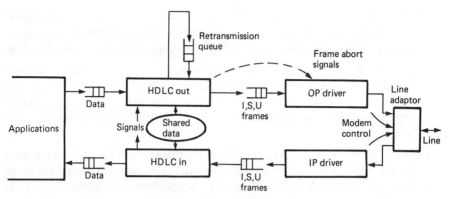

Fig. 5.13   HDLC as two tasks

could be done via a (semaphore-protected) common area. Additionally the input task must be able to *signal* the output task when responses are to be sent and when retransmissions are needed.

On balance it is probably simpler to have *one* HDLC task. The executive is then used to provide task control and scheduling; to support buffer passing and signalling; and to provide interrupt handling for the drivers, if this is not built directly into them.

It should be mentioned that the implementation of a line procedure or protocol, i.e. the obeying of the rules themselves, can often be done in the form of a *state machine* driven from state to state by events. Indeed many communications protocols are *defined* in this form, to make understanding and implementation easy. This topic is returned to in the discussion of X25 levels in Chapter 6.

5.4 The application interface

The interface to the user, the application, provided by communications software should be simple and secure. Often the user is not a sophisticated systems programmer and does not want to learn about (nor can he always be trusted with) semaphore operations, buffer pools, etc. Most commercial real-time operating systems offer users simple interfaces such as Write (message) for output or Read (message) for input. These Write and Read functions are typically subroutines called by the user's code, and therefore logically part of the application task, which interface in turn to the (HDLC) procedure task via semaphores and queues. The handling of these interfaces is built into the subroutines and is transparent to the user.

However, the user must handle his message somewhere. Three approaches are possible:

● The message is in a private buffer, an area in the user's own code module. He passes a pointer to this buffer to the Read or Write subroutines, which arrange, via the driver, for direct input to, or output from, the private buffer from/to the line. In this case there is synchronized input/output, in that the application must wait until the input/output operation has completely finished before it can use its private buffer again. Effectively there is no queuing, unless the application builds its own internal queuing mechanisms.

- The message is in a system buffer. The problem here is that on output the user must GET this buffer for filling before calling WRITE, and on input he must return in (PUT to pool) after READing it. Can he be trusted? Terrible things happen to systems whose buffers are mislaid! What if he overfills a buffer? destroys its header?

- The Read/Write routines *copy* to/from the private buffer from/to the system buffers (which they are responsible for GETting and PUTting). This is the standard approach since it permits unsynchronized input/output, i.e. parallelism, and isolates the application from system resources. It does, however, include the copying overhead.

The design of the user interface is not as simple as indicated. There are other problems we have not faced. How does the user know when to call the Read subroutine if input can be spontaneous, e.g. from a terminal? What information is fed back to the user about errors? Can he simply assume that a message passed for output using Write is successfully sent and received at the remote site, and if not, what then? How does the user activate an input device, e.g. unlock a keyboard, or arrange for a terminal to be included in the polling cycle (Chapter 6)? If different applications share a line, to which one is an input message passed by the communications software? We do not discuss these points further, but suggest that the interested reader looks at the input/output facilities of some commercially available real-time operating systems with these questions in mind.

5.5 Performance

One point about communications software that should be continually stressed is the need for performance. Consider a typical VDU screen capable of holding some 2000 characters, or perhaps many more. At 9600 bps it will take perhaps 2 s to fill it allowing for procedural overheads. This is an acceptable response delay, but only just. Eight seconds, corresponding to 2400 bps, is not. In practice users will want as high-speed lines as possible, and 9600 bps full-duplex implies an input or output character approximately every 400 μs. If interrupts are used there are 2400 interrupts per second per line, in principle.

Interrupt handling alone is likely to take 50–100 μs per interrupt. Rescheduling on every interrupt is clearly unthinkable if a reschedule takes a few hundred microseconds. Communication systems are very heavily loaded. Performance is one of the prime goals of the designer and programmer.

There are various approaches to high performance, all of which are used in effective systems:

- Minimize the traffic. Do not send useless data, e.g. a whole screen-full if only a third of the screen contains information. First clear the screen, then send the data.

- Minimize the instructions executed on each character. Even copying between buffers will use four or five instructions per character, perhaps 2–3% of the time available in our example with only $400\,\mu s$ available per character. Copying, validation, code changing, etc., all take their toll on available time.

- Use appropriate hardware architectures. This approach is obviously open only to those building a new system. However even on normal mini-computers it is possible to get microprocessor-controlled programmable interfaces for a small group of lines. Much of the procedural and driving software can be put into these micros and thus off-load the main computer. This is the *front-end processor* approach.

- Use the hardware facilities available on the devices. In particular terminals with full cursor control and screen-protection facilities (allowing certain fields to be held on the screen and not rewritten on every new output) should be used.

- Plan for overload. The software must not crash when overload occurs. A suitable priority scheme will result in critical code handling input/output always seizing the resources when necessary, leaving less critical code waiting for a lull. In extreme cases overload should be rejected at source. The system should simply reject all new incoming traffic in a way obvious to the originator until the peak is passed. For example, BSC provides a WACK and HDLC an RNR response.

Finally, any buffered system is effectively overloaded when 70% loaded, although this appears to be a contradiction. It arises because queue lengths build up asymptotically at about this level, and although throughput continues, response delays become unacceptable. The ratio of peak to normal traffic flows is often very large, but even if it is only 3 to 1, and we accept that the peak load should not exceed 70%, then the normal load should only be somewhat over 20%. As programmer, designer or purchaser, you have been warned!

5.6 Summary

An approach to handling simultaneous input and output data streams by software (or firmware) has been presented. Many other approaches are possible, but the problems to be tackled and the main strategies for doing so remain unchanged. Mechanisms are required for handling unanticipated input, for supporting parallel activities, and for ensuring the parallel activities can communicate in a non-destructive manner. Clean interfaces must be provided for the user. The software described is very low level, but once the principles are grasped it is relatively straightforward to build large and secure superstructures on sound foundations.

References

1. 'The Design of a Real-Time Operating System for a Minicomputer', Parts I and II,

D. M. Jennings and W. F. C. Purser, *Software – Practice and Experience*, 1975, **5**, 147–67 and 1976, **6**, 327–40.

A more general discussion of real-time software structures, particularly from the language viewpoint, can be found in papers about Modula-2 (e.g. *Modula-2*, N. Wirth, Report 36, Institut für Informatik, ETH, Zurich) or, for example, the *Occam Manual*, Inmos Ltd.

2. *Cooperating Sequential Processes* (F. Genuys (ed.)), E. W. Dijkstra, Academic Press, London, 1968.

3. A particularly well known commercial real-time operating system is Digital Equipment Corporation's 'RSX-11' which exists in various versions. The interested reader is advised to study this and similar offerings from other manufacturers such as Data General, Prime, Modcomp, etc.

4. 'Systems Programming for Data Communication Minicomputers', A. Patel and M. Purser, *Software – Practice and Experience*, 1980, **10**, 283–305.

Chapter 6 Sharing communication lines

Leasing a telephone line is generally less expensive than making dial-up calls if there are more than two or three hours of use, daily, between two points, although this obviously depends on the policies of the PTT in question. (A full economic evaluation would of course include consideration of other solutions, such as use of a packet-switched data network.) Additionally, as we have seen, higher speeds and lower error rates apply on a leased line. But usage in excess of three hours is still much less than 24 hours daily. Moreover, usage is frequently spasmodic, as when a terminal may require to be connected 8 hours per day but only 10 or 20% of line capacity is taken by it, due to pauses by the user at the keyboard. In short, leased lines frequently have much unused capacity. It is logical to consider how this capacity may be made available to other users, to spread the fixed costs as widely as possible.

The basic approach to line-sharing is illustrated in Fig. 6.1. A number of devices, such as terminals, at the remote end are merged onto a single physical circuit by a box which we call a 'channel allocator'. This may be a physical box such as a communications multiplexer or concentrator, or it may be a logical procedure superimposed on simple physical branching as in multidrop lines. At the end local to the (central) computer a similar channel allocator applies. This can be external to the computer, in which case the system usually provides separate channels from the computer to each device, the channel allocators being transparent, or invisible to the computer software. Alternatively the local channel allocator can be implemented, in software usually, within the central computer system, as is the case with multidrop line procedures and sometimes so when a remote concentrator is used.

Line-sharing does not apply only to systems with a single central computer, but this is the basic and typical example which we shall use.

In all cases each remote device has effectively its own *channel* to the central computer via the shared circuit. Two basic approaches to channel allocation are possible:

- Static Allocation, in which each terminal has a fixed portion of the total circuit capacity permanently allocated to it. This privately owned capacity cannot be exceeded by the terminal's traffic; nor can it be re-allocated temporarily to other channels if, for example, the terminal is not currently in use. Static allocation is the technique of Frequency Division Multiplexing

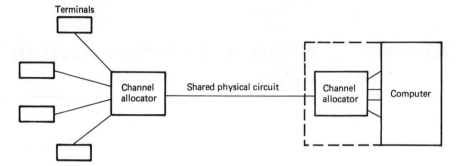

Fig. 6.1   Line-sharing

(FDM), elementary Time Division Multiplexing (TDM) and sometimes of multidrop lines.

- Dynamic Allocation, in which the total capacity of the circuit is dynamically allocated to different channels in response to their traffic needs. This is the technique of more advanced TDM, including Statistical TDM, of concentrators, and usually of multidrop lines. It is also the technique used on access circuits to packet-switched data networks, using protocols such as X25.

In this chapter we first discuss Static Allocation or Static Multiplexing. Then Dynamic Allocation or Dynamic Multiplexing is presented. Finally, because high availability is required in many communications networks, so that multiplexers and concentrators frequently have built-in redundancy, failover and availability for such devices are discussed.

6.1 Static allocation of capacity

6.1.1 Frequency Division Multiplexing (FDM)

The FDM technique is familiar from radio and television. Each sender is allocated a portion of the bandwidth available on the medium, his channel, and he must transmit within that limited frequency range. A receiver must 'tune in' to the frequency he wishes to receive. For transmission in the 'ether' the bandwidth is vast, ranging from tens of kHz to tens of GHz. For leased telephone circuits we are restricted to the usual less than 4 kHz. Additionally, although possible, broadcasting is not usually associated with FDM in data communications, and each channel has normally only one sender and one receiver, both fixed.

Frequency shift keying (FSK) is the usual technique employed. Using this technique, for example, it is possible to fit some 18 75-bps simplex channels onto an unconditioned 2-wire circuit, and perhaps 25 channels if it is conditioned. Each channel is 120 Hz wide, with the logical 1 and 0 coded as frequencies −30 Hz and +30 Hz, respectively, from the centre of the channel. Channel centre-points could be 420 Hz, 540, 660, etc., to 2460, or possibly 3300. Similarly, 300 bps simplex channels of width 480 Hz can be fitted in centred on 1080, 1560,

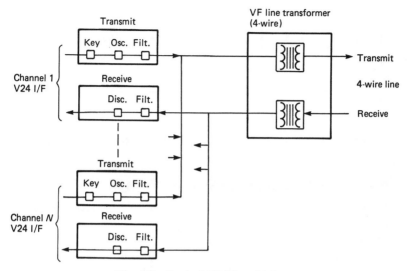

Fig. 6.2 Typical FDM multiplexer

2040, 2520 and 3000 Hz (with conditioning) – i.e. five channels, with logical 1 and 0 − 120 and + 120 Hz from the channel centre. It will be noted that the width in hertz of the channels is 1.6 times the bit-rate supported, which is typical of FSK. In the two examples the aggregate bit-rates are 1875 (75 × 25) and 1500 (300 × 5) bps.

Such an allocation of channels can be used in many ways. We have said that they are simplex. For a full-duplex channel two simplex ones are required. On a real 4-wire leased line each of these two channels would be on a separate unidirectional 2-wire circuit. On a 2-wire leased line this would not be so, and the five simplex 300 bps channels would be reduced to two FDX channels. Again, half-duplex operation on a single channel is obviously possible, provided each end has its transmitter and receiver, as opposed to only one or the other.

In practice such a multiplexer is composed as in Fig. 6.2. A number of V24 interfaces are available, each one being attached to a combined transmit/receive FSK modulator/demodulator, which can be tuned to the frequencies applicable to the configuration. The modulated output/input are merged onto/extracted from the line via a transformer coupling unit. Figure 6.3 shows a typical use of the multiplexer.

It will be appreciated that the FDM technique is simple and that the multiplexer effectively contains its own built-in modems, and so the equipment is, in principle, cheap. On the other hand the technique is inefficient, not only because static allocations of channels is used, but also because aggregate bit-rates on a leased circuit are typically less than 2000 bps, whereas we know 9600 bps can be achieved with good modems.

FDM is thus used on circuits where total traffic flows are relatively low and where cheapness is important. A particularly common application of FDM is carrying many telex channels on a telephone circuit.

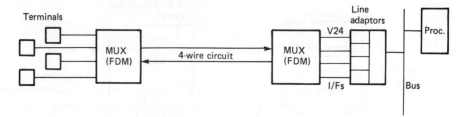

Fig. 6.3   Using a (4-channel) FDM multiplexer. MUX = multiplexer

6.1.2 Basic Time Division Multiplexing (TDM)

Figure 6.4 illustrates the basic TDM technique. Multiplexing is done digitally by taking units of data (bits or octets) from the individual channels and putting them in the *slots* corresponding to those channels in a *time-frame*. The frame is then submitted to a modem and thence to the line. Demultiplexing is the reverse process. The bit-rate on the shared trunk circuit is obviously greater than or equal to the sum of the bit-rates on the individual channels. A 4-wire circuit is used since half-duplex communications is not really feasible because of the delays that would result.

A central problem with basic TDM is the need to maintain synchronism between the low-speed and the high-speed channels. When the moment arrives for a slot corresponding to a specific channel to be transmitted on the high-speed link, data from the low-speed line should be available to put into the slot. The problem of phasing can be overcome by buffering in the multiplexer itself, but there remains the frequency problem. If the unit of data in the slot is an octet (byte), the multiplexer can obviously put in a dummy octet (e.g. a non-printing character) if no real data are available. At the far end the receiving multiplexer can either discard the dummy octet (if it is known never to occur in the real data stream) or it can simply pass it on to the low-speed line, safe in the knowledge that it is ignorable at the application level. However, there are problems if full data transparency is required. This usually only applies to synchronous channels using the multiplexers in which case the protocol operating on the channel will

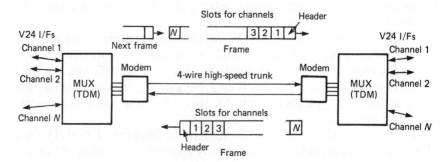

Fig. 6.4   Basic time division multiplexing

hopefully make provision for insertion of extra synchronizing octets, as does BSC with the SYN character.

The problem is more acute if the data unit in the slot is a bit rather than an octet. There is no such thing as a 'dummy bit': it is either 1 or 0. In this case the header of the frame may carry information, effectively stating 'ignore the bit in slot N'. If the header is not to be too long we must ensure that only a few channels are in this state at a time, possibly by more buffering in the multiplexer, at the cost of greater delays. Bit-multiplexing, as it is often called, is usually used only on synchronous channels.

Besides the problem of under-run, when data are not available for a given slot, there is potentially the problem of over-run, when the low-speed channel delivers data faster than the slot rate and exhausts the buffering available in the multiplexer. Over-run usually implies straightforward discarding of characters on asynchronous channels and the abortion of the synchronous block or frame on synchronous channels.

As a result of these considerations, the normal practice for TDM devices is to drive the attached low-speed synchronous channels in strict synchronism with the slot rate using the timing circuits on the V24 interface – in particular circuit 114 (Transmitter Signal Element Timing – DCE Source) – since the multiplexer is effectively a DCE. This ensures that a synchronous block or frame entering the multiplexer at one end of the trunk line emerges from the demultiplexing process at the other end precisely as it entered, i.e. isochronism is maintained. The space between blocks or frames, if not explicitly filled with SYNs (BSC) or Flags (HDLC) by the originator, can be so filled by the multiplexer, provided it recognizes the procedure in use. The approach breaks down with remote connections (Fig. 6.5) in which the low-speed channels are themselves long-distance lines with modems (the remote receiver clock can, with special engineering, be used to provide transmitter clocking), or when a channel is used in half-duplex mode, and the other techniques mentioned earlier must be used. One further method of tackling the problem of synchronous channels is for the multiplexer to recognize and buffer entire blocks/frames, perhaps before or after transmitting them on the trunk circuit, thus ensuring isochronism at the remote receiver. This of course implies more substantial delays.

Thus, whereas it is relatively simple to handle asynchronous channels

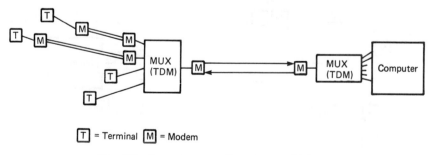

T = Terminal   M = Modem

Fig. 6.5   Remote connections to a multiplexer

carrying plain text using the TDM technique, synchronous channels provide problems. A purchaser of a Time Division Multiplexer should enquire carefully what is meant by 'support of synchronous channels', how that support is achieved, and what are its consequences for performance – in particular, transit delays.

Finally, a well known TDM example, not altogether irrelevant to data communications, is provided by the Pulse Code Modulation (PCM) technique used in telephony. Here, for example, 30 voice channels are sampled 8000 times per second, each sample being a signed 8-bit digital value for the analogue signal. (This is the European (CCITT) standard for PCM. In the USA different rates and framing are used.) A logarithmic scale is used for analogue/digital conversion. The 30 channels are 30 slots in a 32-slot frame running at 2048 kbits, so each channel is effectively 64 kbps. With suitable repeaters (which can be quite widely spaced if optical fibre cables are used) the 2048 kbit stream can be carried in purely digital form. On reception at the user's local circuit digital-to-analogue conversion takes place. Fully digital PCM networks using this TDM technique are in operation in many countries, and the extension of the 64 kbps channel to the user's DTE (telephone that was), as opposed to terminating at his local exchange leaving his local circuit analogue, is also becoming available. Thus data communication users can look forward to modemless 64 kbps digital channels in the relatively near future.

6.1.3 Basic multidrop lines

The basic multidrop configuration is shown in Fig. 6.6. It is centrally controlled by computer software. The computer addresses individual remote DTEs ('terminals') according to a rota, or polling cycle, determined by the software. In the most simple case, rarely seen, static channel allocation would apply; with the computer addressing each remote terminal at fixed intervals, suitably spaced to permit the interchange of the maximum amount of data foreseen.

Two operations are conventionally defined:

- Polling, in which the computer asks a remote-terminal for data. The terminal either responds negatively (there are no data); or sends the data which are

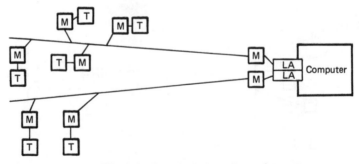

Fig. 6.6   Two multidrop lines

then acknowledged by the computer positively, or negatively if retransmission is required.

- Selection, in which the computer asks a remote terminal if it can receive data. Again, the terminal either responds negatively (if it cannot receive); or positively, and the computer sends the data, and the terminal does the acknowledgement.

In BSC, polling and selection are distinct operations. In SDLC (HDLC), once contacted, a terminal can engage in a full-duplex transfer of information to/from the computer.

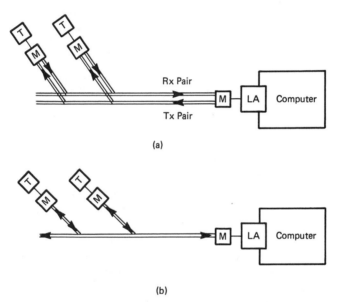

Fig. 6.7   (a) 4-wire multidrop line; (b) 2-wire multidrop line

It will be appreciated that the technique is a form of centrally controlled TDM on a simple infrastructure. That infrastructure usually consists of a 4-wire circuit, one pair used for sending by the computer, the other for receiving (Fig. 6.7a). Branching is either done resistively, to ensure proper balancing of the lines, or with amplifiers. Resistive branching usually allows only four or five branches to be made; amplifier branching might permit 10 or 12. It will be seen that one terminal cannot talk directly to another, as there is no path between the transmitter of one and the receiver of another. Also, whereas the computer can keep its modem's transmitter permanently on (CTS true), the terminals must go through the Request-to-Send process before transmission since they share a common transmit circuit. Figure 6.7b shows a 2-wire multidrop circuit. Here the computer and terminals share the same transmit circuit, and so the Request-to-Send process applies to all of them. However, one terminal *can* talk to another

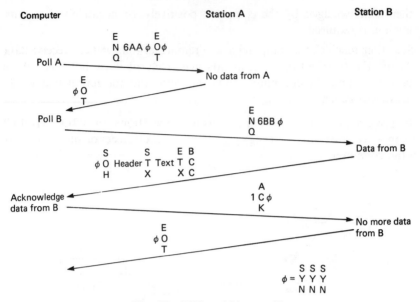

Fig. 6.8   BSC multidrop polling

and, with some ingenuity, the 'turn-to-speak' could be passed directly between them rather than via the central computer.

We shall illustrate the handling of a multidrop line using the familiar BSC [1] procedure (Fig. 6.8) although more elaborate procedures, notably SDLC, do exist. The computer polls station A (address AA) unsuccessfully, since A has nothing to transmit; then station B (address BB) successfully, with B sending one 80-character block – it might send more blocks. The '6' in the poll means 'poll', as opposed to 'select'. The initial EOT sent with the poll, not always necessary, is to tell any currently active terminal to be quiet, i.e. shut off its RTS. When B sends data we have also allowed it to send a header, starting with the BSC character SOH and containing the terminal's identity for confirmation purposes.

Ignoring certain PADding characters, which could apply to give equipment and software time to react, and which are not illustrated, the total number of characters interchanged is 15 (11 + 4) for an unsuccessful poll, and 110 (11 + 90 + 5 + 4) for the successful one. The time taken for this is thus $15/S$ or $110/S$ s, where S is the line speed in characters per second (cps). Additionally CTS (D_{CTS}), propagation (D_P), modem (D_M) and computer/terminal response (D_R) delays also apply; which we shall put at 40, 10 (1000-mile circuit), 2 and 3 ms respectively. When polling, the total time taken, assuming a 4-wire circuit, is thus

$$(1000 \times 15/S + D_{CTS} + 2D_P + 4D_M + 2D_R)\,\text{ms}$$

for unsuccessful polls, and

$$(1000 \times (30 + L)/S + D_{CTS} + 4D_P + 8D_M + 4D_R)\,\text{ms}$$

for successful ones, where L is the amount of data in the block. In our example we have taken $L = 80$ characters, and we take $S = 300$ cps or 2400 bps, so we get:

Unsuccessful poll $= 50 + 40 + 20 + 8 + 6 = 124$ ms

Successful poll $= 367 + 40 + 40 + 16 + 12 = 475$ ms

It will be noted that if 80 characters takes 475 ms, the throughput is 168 cps or 56% of the nominal 300 cps and this takes no account of the potentially long delays between repeated polls of that terminal.

In Fig. 6.9 selection is illustrated. Again we show A replying negatively (NAK) and B positively. The 1 in the initial message from the computer means 'select' rather than 'poll'. It will be seen that the successful selection ends with terminal B still active – hence the initial EOT sometimes necessary, as shown in Fig. 6.8.

The total characters are: Unsuccessful Selection, 15; Successful Selection 107 $(11 + 4 + 87 + 5)$. The times taken are then:

Unsuccessful selection $= 124$ ms (as before)

Successful selection $= 357 + 40 + 40 + 16 + 12 = 465$ ms

Maximum throughput per terminal is obviously dependent on the number of terminals on the multidrop line. If, for example, the procedure polls terminals one by one at 500 ms intervals, and then selects them one by one similarly, and there are N terminals, a complete cycle takes N s. The throughput per terminal is then $80/N$ cps in each direction; and the response time, the time taken for a transaction to/from a particular terminal to be sent, is about $N/2$ s which is the average waiting time of half a complete cycle. This static TDM procedure is clearly

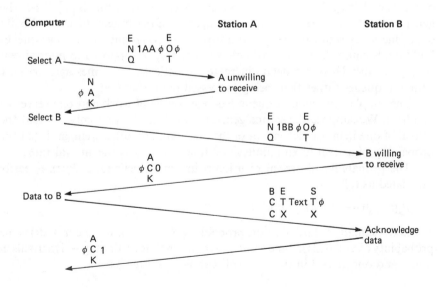

Fig. 6.9 BSC multidrop selection

inefficient. A more dynamic one, in which continuous polling takes place and selection only when required, will, however, have variable throughput and response times depending on the load on the system, the frequency and size of transactions.

6.2 Dynamic allocation of capacity

Since a system which must handle the peak traffic loads on each channel *simultaneously* is naturally built using static allocation (there is no point in being able to allocate capacity dynamically if all peak traffic is already catered for, since there is no extra traffic to which to allocate capacity), systems which employ dynamic allocations always *concentrate*. That is, the sum of the peak traffic loads per channel is greater than the total capacity of the shared trunk circuit. Dynamic systems thus work on the hypothesis that peaks on individual channels do not occur simultaneously, and if and when they threaten to occur some queuing mechanism is available to hold the temporarily delayed traffic. Thus before discussing dynamic allocation we briefly present some elementary queuing theory, which will be used later in analysing the performance, in particular the response times, of systems which allocate channel capacity dynamically.

6.2.1 Elementary queuing theory

We need to consider queuing in data communications, because we are concerned with systems of limited capacity (computers, communication lines) which are being fed with irregular traffic, e.g. messages generated at terminals [2]. When the generated traffic flow rises towards the capacity of the system queues will build up, as messages wait for service. Paradoxically throughput increases as queues build up, because the server has a constant supply, as opposed to intermittent supply of work. However, delays increase dramatically, since messages are now sitting in queues rather than being processed or transmitted.

The simplest model of a queue has one source of work and one server to handle it. We suppose the source generates work items randomly, i.e. that the arrival of one item is independent of the arrival of any other item, and that the probability of arrival in an infinitesimal time is $\lambda \, dt$. λ is the 'arrival rate'.

The probability of arrival of n items in time t, defined as $P_n(t)$, is easily calculated as follows:

$$P_n(t + dt) = P_n(t)(1 - \lambda \, dt) + P_{n-1}(t)\lambda \, dt$$

The above equation states that the probability of n arrivals in time $(t + dt)$ is the probability of n arrivals in time t and no arrivals in time dt, or of $(n - 1)$ arrivals in time t and one arrival in time dt. This can be rewritten as:

$$\frac{dP_n(t)}{dt} = \lambda(P_{n-1}(t) - P_n(t))$$

A solution to this equation is the well known Poisson distribution:

$$P_n(t) = e^{-\lambda t} \frac{(\lambda t)^n}{n!} \qquad (6.1)$$

This satisfies the initial condition

$$\frac{dP_0(t)}{dt} = -\lambda P_0(t)$$

and the basic requirement

$$\sum_{n=0}^{\infty} P_n(t) = 1$$

i.e. that the sum of all the probabilities is unity.

It can be shown that the mean value, or the average number of arrivals in time t, is λt, since

$$\lambda t = \sum_{n=0}^{\infty} nP_n(t)$$

The average time interval between arrivals is therefore $1/\lambda$.

Considering next the server, we suppose an exponentially distributed service time. More precisely, the probability that the service time, s, for an item exceeds t, is given by

$$P(s > t) = e^{-\mu t}$$

where μ defines the rate of service. This exponential assumption is used more for its mathematical convenience than for its verisimilitude. It gives a probability density function, the *a priori* probability that $t < s \leqslant t + dt$ of

$$-\frac{dP}{dt} \cdot dt = \mu e^{-\mu t} \cdot dt$$

In practice service time in computer systems tends to have smallish random variations about a fixed steady mean. However, accepting the assumption, then the probability of service time, s, being less than $(t + dt)$ given that it is greater than t (i.e. the probability of current service ending in the next interval dt) is given by

$$P(t < s \leqslant t + dt \mid s > t) = P(t < s \leqslant t + dt)/P(s > t)$$

$$= \mu e^{-\mu t} dt/e^{-\mu t}$$

$$= \mu \, dt \qquad (6.2)$$

In simple terms, given that an item is being served, it has a constant probability of ending being served in the next infinitesimal time interval.

The average service time is obtained by integrating the product of t and the probability density function $\mu e^{-\mu t}$.

$$\int_0^\infty \mu t \, e^{-\mu t} \, dt = \frac{1}{\mu} \tag{6.3}$$

If $1/\mu$ is the average service time then μ is the service rate.

Looking now at a queue with random arrival rate, λ, and exponential service rate, μ, we can calculate the probability of n items in the system at time t, $Q_n(t)$, as follows:

$$Q_n(t + dt) = Q_n(t)(1 - \lambda \, dt - \mu \, dt) + Q_{n-1}(t)\lambda \, dt + Q_{n+1}(t)\mu \, dt$$

The above equation states that the probability of n items at $(t + dt)$ is that of n items at time t and no arrivals or departures in time dt, or $(n - 1)$ items and one arrival in time dt, or $(n + 1)$ items and one departure in time dt. (More than one arrival or departure has a second order probability and can be ignored.) The formula uses the fact that the probability of leaving the system in time dt is the probability of the current item terminating service, which is $\mu \, dt$: see Equation 6.2. Simplifying:

$$\frac{dQ_n(t)}{dt} = \lambda Q_{n-1}(t) + \mu Q_{n+1}(t) - (\lambda + \mu)Q_n(t)$$

If we assume a steady state has been reached so that the probability of n items is constant, then $[dQ_n(t)/dt] = 0$. This gives

$$\lambda Q_{n-1} + \mu Q_{n+1} = (\lambda + \mu)Q_n$$

Putting $\rho = \lambda/\mu$, a solution to this equation is:

$$Q_n = \rho^n(1 - \rho) \tag{6.4}$$

It satisfies the initial condition

$$\mu Q_1 = \lambda Q_0$$

and the basic requirement

$$\sum_{n=0}^{\infty} Q_n = 1$$

We then have:

$$\text{Average number of items in systems} = \sum_{n=0}^{\infty} nQ_n = \sum_{n=0}^{\infty} n\rho^n(1 - \rho)$$

$$= \frac{\rho}{1 - \rho} \tag{6.5}$$

Although many queuing systems in computers only approximate to the model we have assumed we shall use Equation 6.5 frequently; it is good enough in most practical cases. Note that ρ, which is the ratio of the arrival to the service rate, is called the 'occupancy' and is a measure of load. Note also that we have been concerned with the number of items in the system, which is those in the queue *plus* the one being currently served. Figure 6.10 shows a graph of average

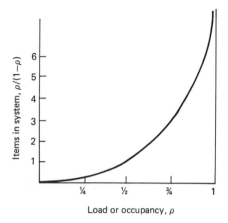

Fig. 6.10 Items in system versus occupancy

number of items in the system against occupancy. The remarks in a previous chapter about loading a system more than 70% will be appreciated now. In systems with queues, a two-thirds occupancy means that the average number of items in the system is 2. An item spends twice as long waiting as being served.

The total average time, waiting plus service, is, from Equations 6.3 and 6.5:

$$\frac{1}{\mu}\frac{\rho}{1-\rho}+\frac{1}{\mu}=\frac{1}{\mu-\lambda} \tag{6.6}$$

A final comment: we have considered only steady-state conditions, when λ and μ are constant and the system has reached equilibrium. The dynamic behaviour of queues, for example if there is a sudden change in λ, is much more difficult to analyse. All that one can say superficially is that a queue will build up rapidly if λ increases, but fall away slowly if λ decreases, for fairly obvious reasons.

6.2.2 Multidrop lines again

Returning to the problem of multidrop lines we now make the assumption of dynamic allocation of capacity. For polling, this is typically achieved by continuous cyclic polling of all terminals. As soon as a terminal which has a message is polled, that message is sent. Obviously the time it takes to get round to a specific terminal is dependent on the traffic offered by the other terminals in the cycle. A queue effectively builds up, although the queue of waiting messages is distributed over the terminals, and usually there can be only one waiting message per terminal.

The waiting time to send an ingoing message is also affected by outgoing messages (selection). With half-duplex protocols outgoing messages are often sent at once, pre-empting the normal cyclic addressing of terminals. The advantage is the reduction in the occupancy of buffers in the central computer. With full-duplex protocols it is usual to wait for the terminal for which the outgoing message is destined to be polled in the normal cycle. Then a full-duplex transfer is possible, assuming an ingoing message is pending. This uses the line more effectively.

As an example, consider a multidrop 2400 bps line, as in the previous example, with eight terminals using BSC. The terminals are supposed to handle 'transactions'. A 'transaction' is defined as an ingoing 40 character message which generates an outgoing 120 character message from the computer. We ask: what is the response time? We define response time as the time elapsed between the ingoing message being ready for transmission at the terminal (operator presses 'Send' key) to the end of reception of the responding message from the computer. We have the following:

$$\text{Response time} = T_P + T_{WIN} + T_{IN} + T_C + T_{WOUT} + T_{OUT}$$

where

T_P = the time awaiting a poll, due to polling of non-sending terminals in the cycle;

T_{WIN} = the waiting time on input caused by transactions to/from other terminals;

T_{IN} = the time to send the ingoing message;

T_C = time taken by computer to process the transaction internally;

T_{WOUT} = the waiting time on output caused by transactions to/from other terminals;

T_{OUT} = the time to send the outgoing message.

The following assumptions are made (see Equation 6.5):

1. $$T_{WIN} = T_{WOUT} = T \frac{\rho}{1 - \rho}$$

where T is the total transaction sending time $= T_{IN} + T_{OUT}$; and ρ is the occupancy of the line.

This assumption states that effectively any ingoing or outgoing message joins a queue of (complete) transactions, waiting on line availability. Of course, the precise waiting time depends on where the terminal is in the polling cycle when the messages to/from it become ready, and on details of the polling algorithm; but assuming the polling algorithm handles all terminals similarly the equation holds for *average* waiting times.

2. $$T_P = T_{POLL} \times \frac{N}{2} (1 - \rho)$$

where T_{POLL} is the time for an unsuccessful poll.

This *ad hoc* equation states that if there is no load then, on average, a terminal waits half a minimal polling cycle, and as the load increases the effect of unsuccessful polls becomes zero – since all are successful.

3. $T_{POLL} = 124$ ms (see example of Section 6.1.3).

4. $T_{IN} = 342$, $T_{OUT} = 598$ ms (easily calculated from the example of Section

6.1.3), therefore

$$T = T_{IN} + T_{OUT} = 940 \text{ ms}$$

5. $T_C = 500$ ms, an arbitrary figure, but which could in principle be calculated knowing what processing was done on the transaction. In particular disk accesses (and queuing for disk accesses!) would enter into this calculation

With these assumptions

$$\text{Response time} = T_P + T_C + T\left(1 + \frac{2\rho}{1 - \rho}\right)$$

$$= 4 \times 124(1 - \rho) + 500 + 940\frac{1 + \rho}{1 - \rho}$$

$$= 496(1 - \rho) + 500 + 940\frac{1 + \rho}{1 - \rho} \text{ ms} \tag{6.7}$$

It remains to calculate ρ. For this we need the traffic flows. Let us assume that a transaction is generated at each terminal at the rate of one every 20 s. Then

$$\rho = \frac{N \times T}{20 \times 1000} \quad \text{(converting ms to s)}$$

$$= \frac{8 \times 940}{20 \times 1000}$$

$$= 0.376$$

$$= 0.4 \text{ approximately}$$

Therefore, from Equation 6.7,

$$\text{Response time} = 0.3 + 0.5 + 2.2$$

$$= 3.0 \text{ s approximately}$$

Ignoring the computer delay, the response time is 2.5 s, which is to be compared with the pure transmission delay, T, of under 1 s. In other words, the load on the line and polling delays introduce queuing delays of about 1.5 s on average.

It can be shown that the variance of the queue length is $\rho/(1 - \rho)^2$ so that the standard deviation is $\rho^{1/2}/(1 - \rho)$. In our case the expected queue length is 0.6 transactions, and the standard deviation is about 1.0, so that the response time is very variable. Additionally many of the assumptions made are questionable, starting from the basic one that there is an exponential service time and including the fact that we have ignored retransmissions due to errors. Nevertheless the calculations do give a useful estimate of *average* response times.

A final comment about the physical configuration of multidrop lines should be made. The analogue branching is of course normally made by the PTTs in, for example, PTT telephone exchanges. Computer suppliers do however provide analogue branching units which can sometimes be used on a large site.

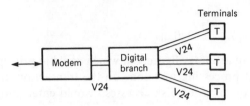

Fig. 6.11 Digital branching

More importantly, they also supply digital branching units (Fig. 6.11). The unit allows the digital (V24) output from one modem to be connected to several local terminals, each via a V24 interface. Traffic for a terminal goes to all terminals so connected, just as with analogue branching; the specific terminals required being picked by the address in the initial poll or select. However, only one terminal may send at a time. This can be forced by some simple logic which ensures that only one CTS is asserted at a time on the V24 interfaces, if through error more than one RTS is present, and TX data are taken only from the terminal to which the CTS is sent.

6.2.3 Dynamic Time Division Multiplexing

Dynamic TDM applies most commonly to asynchronous lines supporting local stop-start terminals (Fig. 6.12). Such 'statistical multiplexers' rely on the fact that:

- some terminals are usually completely inactive at any given time:
- even the active terminals usually use less than 20% of the capacity of their individual lines, when handling interactive traffic.

Thus a statistical multiplexer physically connected to 16 terminals might be programmed (because they are of course microprocessor-controlled) to handle only 12 at a time, by not asserting more than 12 CTS signals in response to RTS signals. Then the frame on the trunk line will be dynamically shared between the 12 active terminals as the needs of the traffic dictate. Each terminal's input (to the terminal) and output circuits will have a buffer for serial/parallel conversion of characters, because a character is usually completely received before forwarding in either direction. In addition, on the output side there will be some more

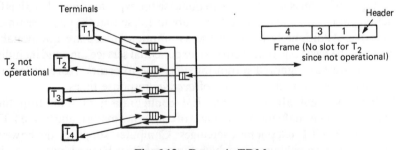

Fig. 6.12 Dynamic TDM

character buffers to hold data until a slot is created for that terminal in the frame on the trunk line. If traffic from several terminals is heavy simultaneously, the trunk line may become temporarily overloaded. In this case, firstly waiting characters accumulate in the output buffers, and secondly the multiplexer may send X-OFF characters to the terminal to tell it to be quiet until it receives an X-ON (assuming the terminal recognizes these characters).

Frequently error detection and correction are available on the trunk circuit, usually by using the conventional HDLC procedure between the two multiplexers, the multiplexing frames now becoming HDLC I-frames. The retransmission delays in case of error obviously increase the multiplexer's buffering requirement. The trunk circuit is often quoted as having an efficiency greater than 100%. This arises as follows. Suppose it runs at 9600 bps = 1200 octets/s. Allowing for framing, other control characters (channel identifiers) and bit-stuffing if applicable, this could reduce to 1100 data octets/s. But if the original characters are 10-bit stop-start characters, the net bit-rate that can be absorbed from low-speed lines is $10 \times 1100 = 11000$ bps. 11000/9600 gives over 110% efficiency!

What is the probability of an overload of the multiplexer? Let us assume that the traffic from all active terminals can be combined to represent a single random source of arrival rate λ cps. The expected number of characters that will arrive in t s is $m = \lambda t$, and the associated variance (from the Poisson distribution, Equation 6.1) is also λt. The probability of more than, say, the capacity arriving in t s is given by

$$\text{Prob}\ (n \geqslant k) = \sum_{n=k}^{\infty} \frac{e^{-m}\ (m)^n}{n!}$$

Figure 6.13 is a Poisson probability chart showing probability on the vertical access, m on the horizontal, and k on a series of curves. (The Poisson distribution is used as an example. For a finite number of inputs other distributions (e.g. the binomial distribution) should strictly apply.)

In our example, suppose the 12 active lines are 2400 bps and provide, on average, 60 cps each; or a combined rate of 720 cps. This can be written as 7.2 characters every 10 ms. From the graph we can see that if the probability of overload in a 10 ms interval is to be kept to less than 1% ($p = 0.01$) then, with $m = 7.2$, k lies between 14 and 15, i.e. approximately double m. Thus the capacity of the multiplexer should be about 1500 cps, which exceeds 9600 bps. In short, overload in a 10 ms interval will occur with greater than 1% probability. If the capacity is actually 1100 cps the probability of overload is more like 10%. Note that the graph is non-linear in the sense that if we consider the probability of overload in a 50 ms interval, in which on average 36 characters arrive, and for which capacity is 55 characters per 50 ms, the probability of overload is reduced to 0.2%. This indicates the importance of buffering to handle very short-duration overloads.

One might estimate buffering capacity as follows. In 50 ms each line can deliver 12 10-bit characters, maximum, so if we provide 12 output buffers to the trunk line per channel, we should certainly be assured of a less than 0.2%

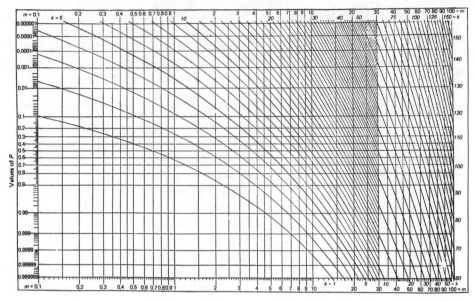

Fig. 6.13 Poisson probability chart

probability of running out of buffers in 50 ms. Looking at this another way, the normal occupancy of the multiplexer of our example is 720/1100, giving $\rho = 0.65$.

It can be shown that the probability of there being k or more items in a system which has a probability distribution given by Equation 6.4, is $p(n \geqslant k) = \rho^k$. In our example with $k = 13$, this probability is under 0.4%. Thus the probability of a queue overflow is very similar to the probability of temporary overload, as previously calculated.

Finally, with $\rho = 0.65$ the average number of characters in the system is about 2. We can then calculate the extra delays introduced in a one-way trip through the multiplexer system, as follows:

$$\text{Delay} = T_{\text{SPS}} + T_{\text{SPF}} \left(1 + \frac{\rho}{1 - \rho} \right)$$

where T_{SPS} is the serial-to-parallel conversion from the slow line, and T_{SPF} is the serial-to-parallel conversion from the trunk line.

Since the slow lines are 240 10-bit cps and the trunk is 1100 cps:

$$T_{\text{SPS}} = 4 \text{ ms}$$

$$T_{\text{SPF}} = 0.9 \text{ ms}$$

So the extra delay $= 4 + 0.9(1 + 2) = 6.7$ ms. This is obviously quite insignificant. With such a fast service rate the problem is not one of delays. The real problem is as discussed earlier: what buffering is required to handle temporary overload?

With dynamic TDM it is possible to handle synchronous channels in one of two ways:

- allocate each synchronous channel its required capacity (static multiplexing) and only perform dynamic multiplexing on the asynchronous channels;
- recognize the protocol on synchronous links, in particular the block structure, so that blocks can be reconstituted on demultiplexing for synchronous delivery to the receiver.

Both approaches were directly discussed under basic static TDM.

6.2.4 Dynamic multiplexing with X25

Some of the problems of handling synchronous traffic with a time division multiplexer have been discussed. However, if one is prepared to multiplex *blocks* of data from different sources, rather than characters or bits, and to accept the resulting delays, multiplexing of synchronous data traffic becomes only a question of defining a block structure and protocol.

Perhaps the best known example of a protocol for the time division multiplexing of many simultaneous conversations on a synchronous line is X25 [3]. The X25 protocol, which first appeared in 1976, was explicitly designed to interface to packet-switched data networks. Since such networks are outside the scope of this book, we do not discuss X25 fully. However, X25 can be, and is, used for multiplexing on ordinary point-to-point links, so a brief description of it is provided here.

X25 is defined in terms of three levels of communication between two end-points; or, strictly speaking, across a DTE/DCE interface. There is the physical level defining the circuits in use; and here full-duplex, synchronous V24 applies, although it is called 'X21 bis'. (The real physical interface is specified by Recommendation X21 of CCITT, but since X21 interfaces are frequently not available, X21 bis is allowed as an alternative.) Above this is the *link level*, which is simply a synchronous line procedure for transferring data packets error-free, full-duplex, between the end-points. The line procedure was originally LAP and then later LAP-B (balanced); i.e. a version of HDLC. HDLC I-frames are used to carry the blocks or packets of data belonging to the third level.

The interesting portion of X25 is level 3, the network level (or layer), which is explicitly concerned with packets. Packets are generated in the computers at the end of the circuit; or perhaps they have been received from a further circuit, and stored in the computer before forwarding on our circuit. Traffic on the circuit is carried on a finite number of logical channels, sometimes called virtual circuits. Each separate conversation is allocated its own logical channel, which, concretely, is identified by a channel number in the packet header. When a new conversation arises it must first establish a logical channel, using the Call Request and Call Connected packets; then it uses the channel by sending Data packets; and finally, when the conversation ends, Clear Request and Clear Confirmation packets are used to free the logical channel.

All packets have a basic header of three octets, identifying the channel number, the type of packet, and that the X25 protocol is in use. Some types of packets have more information in the header and/or a longer header; while the Data packet type obviously has a large data field following the header in which user's data are carried.

A channel is established by one end sending a Call Request packet to the other, on a hitherto free channel. The Call Request packet has several additional fields in the header, which are relevant to networking, such as the final destination address. The receiving end, the Called Terminal, should reply with a Call Accepted packet on the same channel establishing the call; unless there is some reason why the call is unacceptable, in which case the Called Terminal would send a Clear Request packet. (Note that all packets have two names depending on whether they are incoming or outgoing. Thus we have Call Request (Out), Call Indication (In), Call Accepted (Out), Call Connected (In); etc.) In the procedure provision is made for resolving a Call Collision, which could occur if both ends decide that the same channel is free simultaneously, and send opposing Call Requests on it.

Once the caller receives the Call Connected packet the channel is established and caller or Called Terminal can send Data packets on it. To ensure that a single channel does not monopolize the capacity of the circuit, on which other channels are multiplexed, a flow control mechanism exists. This mechanism operates independently on each channel, and in each direction, and ensures that no sender of Data packets can send more than W packets beyond a certain threshold. W is known as the 'window-size', the threshold is the 'window-edge', and the flow control is effected by a receiving end controlling the level of the remote sender's threshold. To facilitate this procedure Data packets have cyclic send-numbers (i.e. modulo-8 or 128), of which sender and receiver must keep track. If a muddle occurs, such as a receiver receiving non-consecutive send-numbers on a given channel, it is possible to Reset the channel. In the data transfer phase there are other packets for flow control and reset, besides those for carrying data. One can also send a very short Interrupt packet, not subject to flow control.

Finally, call clearing is straightforward. Either end can originate the clear by sending a Clear Request packet, to which the correct reply is Clear Confirm.

If X25 is used on point-to-point connections it may well be that only Permanent Virtual Circuits (PVCs) are supported. Such channels do not require to be established and cleared; they exist permanently. For example each logical channel could be mapped directly onto a device or process in the computers at each end of the circuit. Then one would have permanent (virtual) connections between them, multiplexed over the common physical link.

The reader is referred to the CCITT literature for a fuller discussion of X25, but it should be added that although X25 is widely used and accepted, it has had its critics since its inception. Why is the Address Octet of HDLC (X25 level 2) not used for multiplexing, instead of inventing further channels? Surely there is duplication between the error-control mechanism of HDLC and the flow-control mechanism of X25 level 3, both using independent send-numbers? If level 2 provides an error-free medium for level 3, what purpose do Resets serve? These and similar criticisms have been made by many people, and have given rise to alternative, simpler multiplexing protocols [4].

6.2.5 Concentration and protocol conversion

Formerly any device performing dynamic TDM could have made claims to be a concentrator. However, as the power of statistical multiplexers has evolved, the term 'concentrator' has become less clear in meaning. 'Black-box' devices of many sorts are now available, sometimes called 'concentrators', sometimes 'network or communications controllers' (when they include monitoring and control functions), and often 'protocol converters' whose main function is, of course, protocol conversion (particularly on the interfaces to data networks) but which usually have concentration functions also. Rather than discuss all such devices, which would be impossible, we present here, as an example, a particular concentrator.

This concentrator is based on multi-microprocessor hardware with shared memory. The hardware can of course be programmed in many ways. In our example it is designed for an IBM-based SNA (Systems Network Architecture) network. In such a network (Fig. 6.14) a host, front-ended by a 'communications controller', typically handles a collection of multidrop lines to terminal cluster controllers, each of which supports various local terminals. The line discipline is SDLC. The SDLC I-frames carry higher-level commands between host and cluster controller (e.g. for initialization of units and sessions) as well as, of course, data.

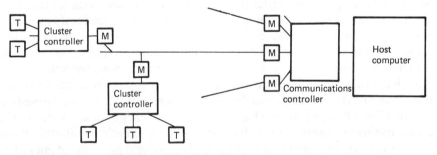

Fig. 6.14 Network without concentrators

The concentrator exists in two versions, local and remote, for interposition in this network (see Fig. 6.15). Its purpose is to allow many remote cluster controllers to share one or two trunk lines between the remote and local concentrators, rather than use a multiplicity of multidrop lines. This can be achieved by dispensing with the capacity consuming polling on the long-distance circuits, and using an efficient point-to-point protocol (HDLC) between the local and remote concentrators. Effectively, a remote concentrator polls the cluster controllers using SDLC. The cluster controllers think they are polled by the host's communication controller. Data from a cluster controller are sent 'spontaneously' through the remote concentrator, up the trunk link, to the local concentrator. The host polls the local concentrator, which appears to the host as many cluster controllers on many multidrop lines.

The concentrator justifies its presence in large systems using long-distance

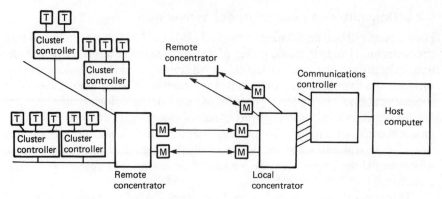

Fig. 6.15 Network with concentrators

lines. Polling and turnarounds are fast on the interface between the local concentrator and host communications controller. Traffic on the long-distance lines is essentially end-to-end data and commands between host and cluster controllers, and line capacity is used far more efficiently than with the polling. Cluster controllers are polled faster and more frequently by the remote concentrators, thus speeding up response. Clearly small delays are introduced in the concentrators in the accumulation of SDLC or HDLC blocks from a line before forwarding, but the faster polling more than compensates for this.

The remote concentrator supports one or two lines to the local one. These can be used for 'traffic balancing' in which data can be sent on either line according to the line loading, as measured, for example, by looking at the queue of buffers awaiting transmission on each line. Full traffic balancing is not usually available; instead each host-to-cluster controller session is allocated the appropriate line when the session is initialized, and all subsequent traffic on that session uses that line. Of course the two lines provide redundancy in case of failures. The concentrators can themselves be duplicated, with automatic monitoring of one by the other (and vice versa), and automatic 'failover' and switching of lines when a failure is detected (Fig. 6.16).

Finally an operator's console can be attached to any concentrator in the network. From it the operator may monitor or control any other concentrator, extracting traffic statistics, recording events, issuing commands to take lines in and out of service, etc. For this to be possible, each concentrator, in particular the local concentrator, has a *switching* function, allowing the operator to establish a 'call' between his console and the desired concentrator.

The concentrators are self-initializing on power-up with regard to their internal configuration and their links to other concentrators. Further initialization information, including the characteristics of the links to the host and to the cluster controllers is obtained from a cassette tape on the local concentrator. Relevant configuration data are *down-line loaded* to the remote concentrators.

Before deciding to use such a concentrator considerable study would be required. On the one hand are the cost items: extra equipment but fewer lines. On the other are the technical considerations: extra capacity and flexibility, changes

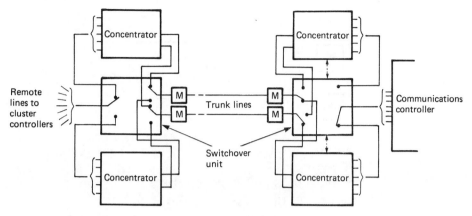

Fig. 6.16 Redundant concentrators and line switching

to response times, vulnerability to failure, etc. Models of loading and queuing in the original and new networks are obviously needed, in which the forecasted traffic loads play a crucial part. The considerations of the previous sections are applicable. Modelling of *availability* is also desirable. This is discussed below.

6.3 Redundancy and failover

Availability calculations are frequently made for computer complexes in which redundant equipment exists [5]. Such complexes have the possibility of automatic failover. This means that a redundant unit is automatically brought into service to replace a unit which was previously in use, but which has failed. We shall apply the theory to communications networks; more particularly, to the extra equipment introduced into Figs. 6.16 and 6.15 in comparison with Fig. 6.14.

The availability of a piece of equipment is defined as the proportion of time for which it is available for use. More precisely, availability is defined as

$$\text{Availability} = \frac{\text{MTBF}}{\text{MTBF} + \text{MTTR}}$$

where MTBF is the Mean Time Between Failure, and MTTR is the Mean Time To Repair.

The MTBF for a unit is usually quoted by a manufacturer on the basis of its internal design and experience with use. Figures of 10 000 to 20 000 h for computer equipment are typical. The MTTR presupposes the presence of someone to effect repairs. Assuming this is so (e.g. with a 24 h on-the-spot maintenance service) a typical MTTR is 1 h. Repairing consists of identifying faulty electronic boards or cards and replacing them. Repairing the card itself is done off-line, probably at a different location.

If a system is composed of two units in series (Fig. 6.17a) with availability A_1 and A_2, the availability of the system is $A_1 \cdot A_2$, since both units must be available for the system to work. If a system is composed of two units in parallel

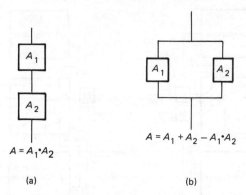

Fig. 6.17 (a) Units in series; (b) units in parallel

(Fig. 6.17b) either of which is capable of maintaining the service of the system, the availability is given by

$$\text{Availability (parallel)} = A_1 A_2 + A_1(1 - A_2) + A_2(1 - A_1)$$
$$= A_1 + A_2 - A_1 A_2$$

since the system is available if both units are available, or if one and not the other, or if the other and not the one. It is possible to build availability diagrams. Figure 6.18 shows availability diagrams for a host-to-cluster controller link corresponding to Figs. 6.14, 6.15 and 6.16 respectively. The diagrams only consider equipment external to the host's communications controller and the cluster controller; and in the case of Figs. 6.18b and 6.18c, the very short link to the local concentrator is ignored. The diagrams are to be read as a chain of items of known availability, and we are concerned with the availability of a path through the chain.

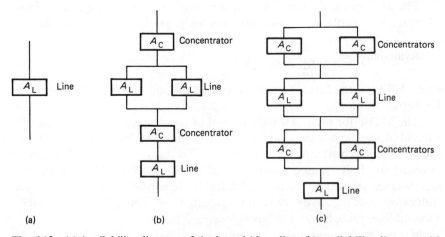

Fig. 6.18 (a) Availability diagram of single multidrop line; (b) availability diagram with concentrators and dual trunk line; (c) availability diagrams with dual concentrators and dual trunk line

For example, the following assumptions are made:

- Redundant lines or units have the same availability, A, so that the availability of two units in parallel is $2A - A^2$.
- The MTBF for concentrators is 20 000 h, and the MTTR is 1 h, so the availability of a concentrator, A_c, is 0.99995.
- The availability of a remote communications link, including its modems, is independent of its length.

As an example, a method of estimating the availability of a communications link, knowing how it is handled by software, is briefly presented.

Suppose a link runs at N bps with a bit error rate B. Then the expected number of errors in S s is $S \cdot N \cdot B$. We shall assume that if the software detects an average bit error rate in excess of 10^{-3} (1 in 1000) over 5 s it determines that the line is unavailable. It will try using the line again at intervals of 30 s. In this case the MTTR = 30 s, and the MTBF is 5/(Probability of unavailability) s. The probability of unavailability is the probability of more than k bit errors in 5 s, where $k = 5N \cdot 10^{-3}$, given that the mean $m = 5N \cdot B$. We can use the Poisson graph of Fig. 6.13 to read off this probability.

If, for example, a line has $N = 2400, B = 2 \times 10^{-4}$, then $k = 12, m = 2.4$ and the probability of unavailability is 0.00001, so the MTBF = 5×10^5 s or some 140 h. Again, if $N = 9600, B = 5 \times 10^{-4}$, then $k = 48, m = 24$, and the probability of unavailability is also about 0.00001. We shall assume that the multidrop lines in our example are 2400 bps with BER = 2×10^{-4}, and the trunk lines are 9600 with BER = 5×10^{-4} so they both have availability, A_L,

$$A_L = \frac{500\,000}{500\,030} = 0.99994$$

Applying these assumptions to the three cases we have:

1. No concentrators (Figs. 6.14 and 6.18a)

    Link availability = $A_L = 0.99994$

2. Non-redundant concentrators with redundant trunk circuits (Figs. 6.15 and 6.18b)

    Link availability = $A_c \cdot (2A_L - A_L^2) \cdot A_c \cdot A_L$

    $= 0.99984$

3. Redundant concentrators with redundant trunk circuits (Figs. 6.16 and 6.18c)

    Link availability = $(2A_c - A_c^2)(2A_L - A_L^2)(2A_c - A_c^2) \cdot A_L$

    $= 0.99994$

If the assumptions about the basic figures for availability of individual items are correct, it is clear that the configurations of 1 and 3 give the same availability of some 6 h downtime in 100 000, or $\frac{1}{2}$ h/year; while configuration 2 has a downtime of $1\frac{1}{3}$ h/year. However, many people might question the figure of 0.99994 availability as calculated here for a line. It takes no account of prolonged outages due, for example, to cable or exchange faults.

It should be added that the calculations have not included loss of availability owing to the time it takes to switch over units when failure occurs. Nor have they included the reliability, or otherwise, of the failover mechanisms themselves. Typically, failover is effected by a combination of software and hardware. Each unit of a redundant pair monitors the other, by sending a message to it at a regular frequency and checking the reply. If the non-active one fails to get the reply, it assumes the active one has failed and takes control by issuing a command to the hardware switchover unit. If the active one fails to get a reply from the non-active one, it knows that no stand-by is available for failover and advises the network operator accordingly.

Another approach is for the switchover unit to receive regular messages from each principal unit. If these fail, the switchover unit draws its own conclusions and switches lines appropriately.

Yet a third approach is for each unit to have its own 'watchdog' timer which must be reset regularly. If it is not reset, the watchdog automatically triggers the switchover unit to act.

Finally, more ambitious approaches to failover are possible in which both units are always operational, rather than one in a stand-by mode. In this case, for example, both units would process all incoming traffic, but only one would generate outgoing traffic. If that one fails the other can, in theory, take over at once. Short of rigidly synchronizing the two units (as indeed is sometimes done) such an approach is liable to create serious software problems.

We conclude this chapter by illustrating (Fig. 6.19) a much simpler and very

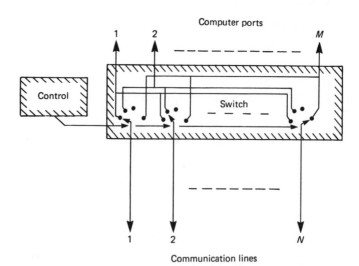

Fig. 6.19   Line switching at entry to computer. Note: control ensures that no two of the N communication lines are connected to the same port out of the M ports available

common switching device for communication lines. Basically it enables any line to be connected to any computer port, of one or more computers. It can be controlled perhaps manually with jacks, or manually from a terminal, or automatically by commands from the host computer.

References

1. *General Information – Binary Synchronous Communication.* IBM GA27-3004.

2. A good simple introduction to Q theory is *Queues*, D. R. Cox and W. L. Smith, Chapman and Hall, London, 1974.

3. *Recommendation X25*, CCITT Red Book, Fasc. VIII.3.

4. 'The PHS Protocol', Purser, Horn and Sheehan in *Software – Practice and Experience*, 1984.

5. *Reliability: Management, Methods and Mathematics*, D. K. Lloyd and M. Lipow, Prentice-Hall, Englewood Cliffs, NJ.

Chapter 7 Networks without switching – LANs

In the previous chapter it was shown how many channels, for example linking terminals and a host computer, could share a single physical circuit. A host supporting several such shared circuits is the hub of what is often called a 'star network', although there is in general no 'net' but rather a multiplicity of channels diverging from a single centre. Two or more host computers could share a circuit, using for example a time division multiplexer (Fig. 7.1), but this is still not really a network: it is a collection of point-to-point channels, albeit of some complexity. Without a reconfiguration, DTE A always talks to DTE B; and reconfiguration is performed by a network controller, not by the ordinary user.

Most people would consider that for a mesh of interconnections to be called a network it should have the property of *switching*. That is, DTE A can send data to DTE B or DTE C, using a single channel on DTE A's interface to the network, provided DTE A gives the network some suitable instruction as to the required destination. This is how the telephone network functions: firstly the user selects the destination (dialling), then he exchanges information with that destination. In such a network there is what we shall call 'active switching', since the network actively makes the connection. Such active switching networks are outside the scope of this book.

Another simpler but yet familiar form of selecting a destination may be called 'passive switching' or 'selective broadcasting'. Here the sender's message goes to *all* destinations, but only a few (usually one) are designated to receive it. There is a real network, since any DTE can reach any other DTE in principle, but the network really performs no switching – hence the title of this chapter.

Multidrop lines are a primitive example of this passive switching technique, since the host's polling and selection messages go to all terminals, although only one is supposed to respond. However they are very limited, because there is no means for directly connecting two terminals together. Of course terminal A could send a message to terminal B if the central computer is programmed to act as a switch; but this is really switching *externally* to the network.

7.1 Passive switching

Proper examples of passive switching or selective broadcasting are provided by Local Area Networks (LANs) and satellite-based networks. These function using a form of dynamic time division multiplexing, in which the would-be sender

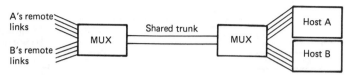

Fig. 7.1   Two hosts share a trunk circuit

has to acquire a time-slot on the broadcasting medium (cable, satellite channel, etc.) and then send its message in that time-slot. The message will contain the identification of the required destination(s). These networks may therefore also be called Time Division Multiple Access (TDMA) networks. (We do not consider schemes involving frequency division multiplexing, as are sometimes used on broadband networks based on cable-TV technology, as passive switching networks [1]. Normally no switching is possible, since source-destination pairs are fixed; or, if switching is possible, it is at the centre of a single star network and is more in the nature of a reconfiguration.)

TDMA networks are basically of two types:

1. those in which slots are explicitly offered to potential senders, who then use them, safe in the knowledge that they are theirs, or decline them;

2. those in which would-be senders seize apparently vacant slots and start transmitting. However, a sender will also have a collision-detecting (CD) mechanism to enable it to see if the slot was simultaneously seized by another sender. When a collision is detected appropriate recovery action must be taken.

This chapter reviews some TDMA schemes for LANs, and concludes by considering software for LANs. The discussion of satellite-based networks is deferred to the next chapter.

7.1.1 Local area networks

Figure 7.2 illustrates a typical Local Area Network (LAN). A common highway, a cable, links together all DTEs. This cable may be closed in a loop, in which case data are usually sent in one direction only round the loop; or it may be open-ended with suitable terminations. Devices connect to the cable via what we shall call nodes. A node has one (or possibly more than one) address to identify it to the network. A node recognizes the formats of traffic on the network, and obeys and generates commands and responses in those formats, received from or sent to other nodes. Transmission on the network is bit-serial, and usually at high data rates to permit time division multiplexing of many channels, e.g. in excess of 1 Mbps.

A node provides one or more standard interfaces to attached devices, DTEs. As with all real networks, DTEs must conform to the network, rather than the network to the DTEs. Thus for a device to be attachable to the LAN it will require some interfacing card which will plug into its own internal bus, or equivalent, and present the standard interface for connection to a node. This standard interface

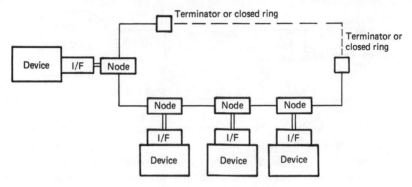

Fig. 7.2   A generalized LAN

we call the *device interface*. It is usually a parallel interface, with octets transferred across it as eight parallel bits. The device interface is not necessarily very high speed since:

- the raw bit-rate of the LAN is reduced by the removal of control and other bits by the node, which only passes data bits, and those in parallel, to the device;

- only a fraction of the total data traffic on the LAN passes to/from any particular device;

- the node usually provides buffering, and sometimes flow-control mechanism, to absorb or block any data flows which a device cannot sustain.

Data are usually transmitted on the network in the form of packets. A packet is a block of data in an envelope of control and other bits; analogous, for example, to an HDLC I-frame. A packet will normally include at least the address of the required destination node on the LAN. A LAN may have a fixed packet size, a fixed maximum packet size, or an unrestricted packet size. However, since the packet size determines the time-slot required by the packet on the network, it is clearly undesirable to have very large packet sizes, since other users would be penalized. Packets need not necessarily always carry data. The essential functions of a node are thus to extract data from packets addressed to it on the LAN, and pass the data to its attached device(s); and to build addressed packets from data received from the device(s), and transmit them on the LAN.

The LAN is usually a few hundred metres in length, and at most a few kilometres. LANs can be interconnected by bridges or *gateways* (Fig. 7.3) for the purpose of further extension, or perhaps by simple signal repeaters, but performance may suffer on overextended networks, depending on the techniques used. Because of its high bit-rate, a LAN may have a significant number of bits in transit. For example a 1 km length of cable can hold some 45 bits if the bit-rate is 10 Mbit/s. In some LANs the stations contain repeaters which have buffering for a few bits, so the number of bits in transit is further increased.

Where are LANs useful? Whenever there is a requirement for a fully connected network (in which any DTE can access any other directly) within a

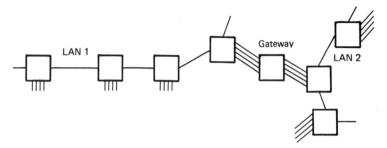

Fig. 7.3 A gateway between two LANs

limited area, a LAN is attractive. If there are N DTEs only one cable is required instead of $N(N-1)/2$, and each DTE requires only one interface instead of $(N-1)$. The requirement or full connectivity is not very common, but many systems do need a relatively high connectivity; for example, a computer complex in which all processors must be able to communicate with each other, all terminals must be able to access all processors, and several processors must share devices such as printers, plotters or filestores. The LAN itself of course costs money: its nodes, its cable. This cost must be offset against the savings in cabling and interfaces mentioned above. In particular, the interfaces 'saved' and the software to drive them may actually be cheaper and more readily available than the device interfaces to the LAN which replace them. There is also a question of reliability. If the LAN fails all communication fails. That is why proponents of passive LANs, such as Ethernet [2], in which the LAN itself contains no active components, consider their systems superior to LANs which require an active controller. In all cases the nodes will contain active components, but a well designed LAN will be such that failure of a single node affects neither the LAN itself nor other nodes.

Although one might expect the question of capacity to figure highly in assessing a LAN, practical experience has shown that very few LAN-based systems, even under peak traffic conditions, load the LAN more than say 15 or 20% – always assuming the LAN speed is in the Mbit/s range. This is essentially because traffic is limited by the speed of computer programs, or by electro-mechanical devices such as printers, or by users, for example at terminals.

Finally, LANs can serve a very useful purpose in interfacing a computer complex to a high-speed long-distance circuit, such as might be provided by a satellite link, or a 2 Mbit/s optical fibre circuit (Fig. 7.4). In this case the LAN effectively acts as a multiplexer/demultiplexer to/from the long-distance circuit. It assumes, of course, that a suitable high-speed interface between the LAN and the long-distance circuit can be built – a non-trivial task, particularly when software is involved.

7.1.2 Token-passing and empty-slot LANs

One class of LANs which uses the first TDMA approach discussed earlier, in which the right to transmit is explicitly given to a node, is that based on token

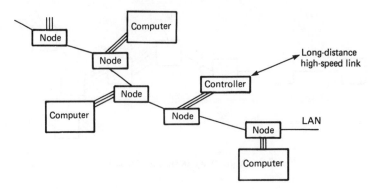

Fig. 7.4   A LAN as a multiplexer onto a high-speed link

passing. The 'token' is the right to transmit. The technique supposes that someone gives the node the token. The giver can be either the previous holder of the token, or a central control node (a *Monitor*), or perhaps some combination of these approaches. In any case the functioning of the LAN is dependent on the correct functioning of the giver, thus creating a potential reduction in reliability. Various token-passing LANs exist or are in development, in particular IBM's offering. One such token ring procedure is presented in Chapter 8 under the heading of satellite access control.

A special form of token passing delivers not only a token but also the 'vehicle' in which to transmit data, an empty packet. The Cambridge Ring [3] is the best-known example of such a LAN. It is briefly presented in what follows. The version is that of Polynet [3].

The Cambridge Ring is a circular, unidirectional LAN in which minipackets (so-called because a minipacket only carries two octets of data) circulate continuously. It is controlled by a Monitor (Fig. 7.5), which ensures that an integral number, N, of minipackets plus a Gap are in circulation, by having appropriate buffering and synchronizing mechanisms. The value of N depends on the physical extension of the Ring, and the number of nodes on it, and is determined by the Monitor on initialization.

The purpose of the Gap (which contains all bits set to zero) is to allow the Monitor to check the minipacket structure, and to permit some flexibility in the configuration. The Gap is usually less than a minipacket in length. A minipacket contains a Full bit, set to 1 when it contains data. It also contains two Response bits set to 11 when the minipacket is loaded with data. When the minipacket reaches the destination node four things can happen:

- The two data octets are read, and the two Response bits are set to 10.
- The node is busy and cannot read the data. The Response bits are set to 00.
- The destination node refuses to accept data from the source node. The Response bits are set to 01. (This could occur if the destination node has been commanded by its associated device to receive data only from some specified source, which is not the actual sender.)

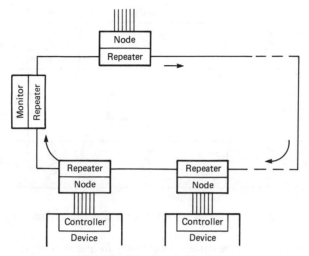

Fig. 7.5 The Cambridge Ring

● Nothing. The destination does not exist or is inactive. The Response bits remain at 11.

The minipacket also contains a Monitor bit, set by a source when filling the minipacket, and cleared by the Monitor when the minipacket passes it. (Since any full minipacket returns to its source round the Ring, which then notes what happened to it from the Response bits and marks it as Empty, a full minipacket with the Monitor bit equal to zero arriving at the Monitor is an error – it is going round full the second time. The Monitor marks such minipackets as empty again.) No node may use the same minipacket for sending on two successive circulations. Additionally, a station which wishes to send is prohibited from using the next minipacket, if empty, after receiving a returned full one, to prevent it monopolizing Ring capacity.

The minipacket format is shown in Fig. 7.6. The first, Start (S) bit is always 1. The Destination address (DST) and Source address (SRC) octets identify the corresponding nodes. The two Type bits (T) are for the users, the communicating devices, to qualify the minipacket – see below. The Maintenance (M) bit is an even parity check on the minipacket. The format illustrated is that of the later 40-bit rather than the earlier 38-bit minipacket.

A source node which receives a Busy response from the Destination can

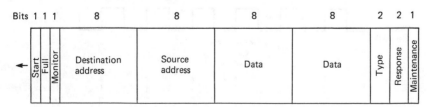

Fig. 7.6 Minipacket format (Cambridge Ring)

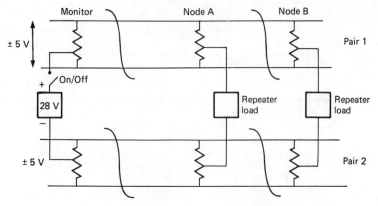

Fig. 7.7 Power distribution on a Cambridge Ring

contain an automatic retry feature, at decreasing frequencies, to avoid loading the attached device with retries. A source can also broadcast to all destinations, using a special destination address, in certain implementations (e.g. Polynet). In this case the Response bits are not used. Another special destination address may be used for Fault-reporting minipackets, generated by a node essentially for transmission to the Monitor. Finally, a node can temporarily select a unique source from which it will receive data, as discussed previously.

Physically the Ring normally consists of repeaters linked together by two telephone pairs, although optical fibre links are also possible. Each pair carries digital signals at the 10 Mbit/s rate, represented as ± 5 V between the wires of the pair. One pair is centred on the positive side of a 28 V source, the other on the negative side. This power is injected at the monitor and is used by the repeaters, which do not require a local power source. See Fig. 7.7. The encoding of data is shown in Fig. 7.8. A transition on one pair signifies 0. A transition on two pairs signifies 1. No transition on either pair is an error. Since there is always a transition if there is no error, the network effectively is transmitting a clock signal, used by all repeaters.

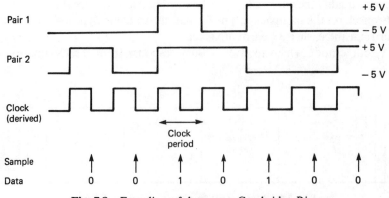

Fig. 7.8 Encoding of data on a Cambridge Ring

Repeaters may be free-standing or incorporated into a node. The maximum distance between repeaters is less than 200 m. A node always contains a repeater, powered from the Ring, plus the node's own logic (powered locally), whose function it is to handle minipackets destined to it, and to inject data into free slots when it wishes to send. This is essentially done by shifting the minipacket into a receiver in the node and, if necessary, shifting a new minipacket onto the Ring from a transmitter in the node (see Fig. 7.9). The sequence of bits in the minipacket is obviously designed to simplify the procedure. For example, the fact that the first bit (after the S-bit) is the Full bit, allows a receiving node to decide at once whether this minipacket is available for transmission or not; and, if it is, to start shifting out any minipacket it has awaiting transmission.

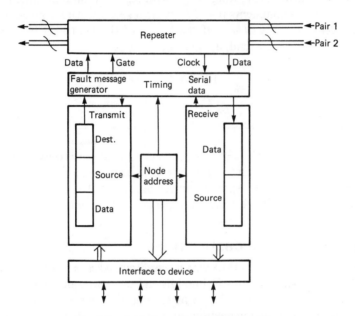

Fig. 7.9 A node on the Cambridge Ring

There are various error-checking features in the Ring. The use of the Monitor has been mentioned, and the existence of the Parity bit. Any node receiving a minipacket with an erroneous Parity bit corrects it and sends a Fault-reporting minipacket in the next empty slot. Similarly, a Fault-reporting minipacket is sent if a node ceases to receive clocking from the Ring. Thus the node downstream of a break or other fault will immediately begin advising the Monitor. Additionally, the Monitor fills empty minipackets with random bit patterns, and checks them when they return after a cycle. All sending nodes also check the data in a returned minipacket. Finally, nodes identify returning minipackets by counting those in circulation, not by looking at the (possibly corrupted) source address.

How is the Ring used by software? Since a minipacket carries only two octets, any normal block sent from device A to device B via the Ring will require many minipackets. A mechanism is required to indicate the start and end of blocks. The Type bits can be used for this. Provided that a given source A can only send one block at a time to a given destination B, there is no need to identify within each minipacket what block it belongs to: that is implied by the source and destination addresses. A device may contain various 'processes'. By associating 'ports' within a node with each process, and including the port number(s) in the block header it is possible for example to multiplex conversations between any given pair of devices at the block (but not at the minipacket) level. If required, a block can contain sumcheck characters. In any case some basic rules will be required in the devices to govern the handling of incomplete or corrupted blocks, etc. In fact such a set of rules does exist and is known as the Basic Block Protocol (BBP) [4].

A final comment on the Ring is also with regard to multiplexing. It will be clear from previous comments that if N minipackets circulate, a given node can only send once in every $N + 2$. If the length of the Gap is G bits, then the maximum bit-rate, S, for sending *data* at a node is

$$S = \frac{16}{40} \times \frac{40}{(N + 2)40 + G} \times 10^7 \text{ bps}$$

$$G = \frac{16 \times 10^7}{40N + G + 80} \text{ bps}$$

For $N = 1$, ignoring G, $S = 1.3$ Mbps. Since a single node only takes one slot in three, three nodes can send at this rate at once, giving a total of 4 Mbps. In general, the total maximum throughput remains fixed at about 4 Mbps as slots are added, but the available bandwidth per node decreases.

7.1.3 Seizing slots and CSMA-CD

In the second approach to TDMA which was discussed earlier, a user wanting to transmit seizes apparently unused timeslots and starts sending data. In a variant of this technique, used on LANs, a node simply listens to activity ('Carrier Sensing') on the broadcasting medium, and when there is silence assumes it may transmit. There are no regular slots. Such systems are known as Carrier Sense Multiple Access with Collision Detection (CSMA-CD), because of course they include a mechanism for resolving contention between two or more nodes for the medium. The best-known example of a CSMA-CD system is Ethernet. What follows is a brief description of Ethernet taken from the *Blue Book* published by the Digital Equipment, Intel and Xerox Corporations [5].

Ethernet is based on a coaxial cable, not in a ring, to which nodes are connected. A coaxial cable segment is less than 500 m in length, although the segments may be interconnected by repeaters provided that the total length is less than 1500 m. A node consists of a *Transceiver* on the cable connected via a transceiver cable to a *Control Board*. In turn, the control board connects to the user device or 'station', typically plugging in directly to the device's bus (see Fig. 7.10).

The Carrier Sense signal is generated in the control board on the basis of

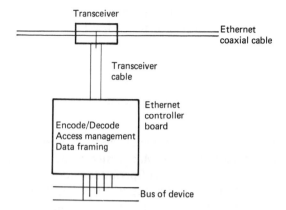

Fig. 7.10 Interfacing to Ethernet

information received from the transceiver. A station that wishes to transmit will do so if Carrier Sense is false, i.e. no other node is transmitting. If Carrier Sense is not false, a would-be transmitter must wait until it is false, plus a further 9.6 μs to provide interframe spacing.

The unit of transmission is the frame, whose format is illustrated in Fig. 7.11. A frame contains a 4-octet destination address, a 4-octet source address, 2 octets to denote the frame type, a data field of 46–1500 octets in length, and a 32-bit CRC. The destination address selects the destination node. The source address is inserted automatically into the frame but is not used by the destination node; instead it is passed up to the user program at the receiver. Similarly the type octets are not used by Ethernet but passed between users, for example to identify what procedures or protocols may apply between two correspondents. The data field allows complete transparency. The 32-bit CRC is used for error detection and is based on the generating polynomial

$$G(x) = x^{32} + x^{26} + x^{23} + x^{22} + x^{16} + x^{12} + x^{11} + x^{10} + x^8 + x^7$$
$$+ x^5 + x^4 + x^2 + x + 1$$

The CRC procedure is similar to that for HDLC: the shift registers are preset to all 1s; the CRC is complemented before transmission; the received CRC is passed through the calculating mechanism, and a fixed result (11000111 00000100 11011101 01111011) is obtained if there is no error.

A frame is preceded by a preamble of alternating 1s and 0s, to allow receivers to reach a steady state. The end of the preamble is denoted by two consecutive 1s, the total length being 64 bits. There is no need for the frame format to make

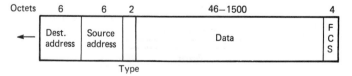

Fig. 7.11 An Ethernet frame

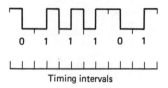

0 1 1 1 0 1

Timing intervals

Fig. 7.12 Manchester encoding on Ethernet

provision for identifying the end of frame, as this is signalled by failure of Carrier Sense. The mechanism is as follows. Manchester encoding is used for the bit-stream in which a 1 is coded as one half-period low-level followed by one half-period high-level signal, and a 0 as the opposite (see Fig. 7.12). As a result, when transmission is in progress there is at least one transition (high/low or low/high) for each bit. Termination of transmission can be then determined immediately – in practice 1.6 bit times (160 ns).

The preamble and frame are passed serially from the control board to the transceiver for emission onto the coaxial cable. At the receiving node, the transceiver routes the frame serially into the control board for handling. The transceiver is thus linked to the control board by two twisted pairs for transmission and reception, transformer-coupled to the coaxial cable. Additionally the transceiver signals the control board when it detects a *collision* on the network, via a third twisted pair; while a fourth pair feeds the transceiver with power (Fig. 7.13).

The transceiver detects a collision from voltage abnormalities on the coaxial cable. A collision can occur within a *collision window*, which is the time elapsed between node A starting to send a frame and the start of A's frame reaching node B (just after B has started sending); plus the delay in the start of B's frame reaching A. The collision window is thus the maximum round-trip delay on the network, of the order of 45 μs for the largest permitted Ethernet configurations.

If a transceiver detects a collision it signals the control board accordingly. If that node was also transmitting it signifies that its transmission has been corrupted. It must then cease transmission, *back-off* and retry. Before retrying the node *enforces* the collision by sending an arbitrary bit pattern of 32–48 bits in length, the *jam*, to ensure that other nodes involved in the collision notice it. The back-off interval before the retry is random in length, and expanded on each retransmission attempt, to reduce the load when the network is busy.

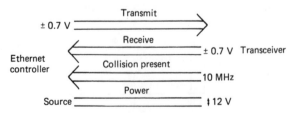

Fig. 7.13 Ethernet transceiver cable

Ethernet specifications are for:

- the coaxial cable and its connection mechanisms;
- the interface between the transceiver and the control board, the transceiver cable;

(the above two are physical specifications)

- the logical handling of frames by the control board, including frame format, rules for transmission, reception and collision handling.

The basic specifications do not provide for any frame acknowledgement, as for example in HDLC. A control board can recognize a frame with a CRC failure, and similar errors. It delivers the received frame to the user with the corresponding status information (receive OK, frame check error, alignment error – e.g. not an integral number of octets in the frame). It is left to the user to recover from these error situations.

7.1.4 Comparison of Ethernet and the Cambridge Ring

Comparing Ethernet with the Cambridge Ring we may note the following points:

- Ethernet uses a passive medium; it does not rely on an active monitor. Therefore it is potentially more reliable.
- Ethernet becomes inefficient as it is loaded up (since the probability of collision increases), as it is extended in length (because the collision window becomes larger), and particularly when frames are short. A heavily loaded Ethernet, with average frame duration equal to the collision window, has an efficiency of $1/e$ (e = base of natural logarithms) [2]. This is not the case with the Cambridge Ring, whose efficiency is almost constant.
- Ethernet's physical extension is more limited than that of the Ring, because of loss of efficiency consequent on propagation delays. Both systems require repeaters for larger networks. The Ring requires additional power input as well as more frequent repeaters, when extended.
- Ethernet's addressing system permits many more nodes than that of the Ring.
- Basic Ethernet supports no acknowledgement of reception of packets. The Cambridge Ring has acknowledgement only of 2-octet minipackets. Both systems need some superior protocol.

7.2 Software and LANs

There are two ways of viewing LANs when considering software. The first is to consider them as just normal intercomputer serial links, albeit with special characteristics such as fast response, and high throughput. In this view, any application above the basic link protocol (such as the Cambridge Ring's BBP) can ignore the underlying technology and act as though its interlocutor across the

LAN were on a conventional point-to-point connection. We do not discuss this view further.

The second way of looking at LANs starts from the observation that it is possible to send a short message, say 2 octets, across the LAN in less than 10 μs. (For example on the Cambridge Ring Access Time $= \frac{1}{2}$ slot, Transmission Time $= 1$ slot, Propagation Time $=$ perhaps $\frac{1}{2}$ slot, Total $= 2$ slots $= 8$ μs.) When we consider that rescheduling a computer, because a message has been passed between two tasks within it, can take several hundred microseconds, it is apparent that tasks running on distinct computers communicating across a LAN can be in almost as close communion as distinct tasks within the same computer. It becomes possible to consider a collection of programmable processors, interconnected by a LAN, as a unit, running under a single distributed operating system.

What would such an operating system look like? What follows is a description of the kernel of a distributed operating system based on the discussion of Chapter 5. Recapitulating, the kernel is concerned with multitasking and supporting intertask communication. Three types of intertask communication exist: via shared memory, signalling, buffer passing. On this foundation the most elaborate real-time system can be built.

In our distributed operating system we eliminate shared memory as not applicable to LANs, since software on one computer cannot access memory on another across the LAN without co-operation from software *within* that other computer. This leaves signalling and buffer passing. Signalling is handled by p- and v-operations on semaphores (which can also be used to control access to shared resources such as a device accessible across the LAN), buffer passing by Put and Get operations. We assume each computer on the LAN is running the kernel we have described, supporting its own internal multitasking. The objective is to extend the four VIs p (semaphore), v (semaphore), PUT (Queue) GET (Queue), so that they can operate on semaphores or queues not local to the processor in which the calling task is running.

The approach is as follows:

1. The four VIs are modified to include a check on whether the target entity (Semaphore, Queue) is local or not. This can be done by table look-up at run-time. If the target is not local, the VI builds an appropriate command in a SEND buffer which is put to the (local) LAN output driver for sending. In the cases of the p-operation and GET, the calling task is suspended and the processor is rescheduled (see Fig. 7.14). (An alternative approach, if target entities are known at compile-time, is to perform the local/remote check on compilation and arrange for the corresponding version of the VI to be called.)

2. The LAN output driver is a conventional looping driver (Fig. 7.15) getting a SEND buffer, emptying it to the LAN (probably not under interrupt control since the inter-octet interval is too short), returning the empty SEND buffer to a pool, and repeating. The SEND buffers hold either very short commands, e.g. specifying p-op, semaphore and destination processor; or include a data portion also, e.g. for PUT.

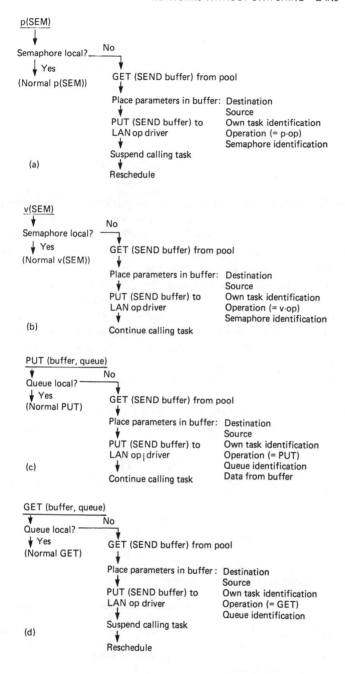

Fig. 7.14 (a) p(SEM) operation for LAN; (b) v(SEM) operation for LAN; (c) PUT operation for LAN; (d) GET operation for LAN

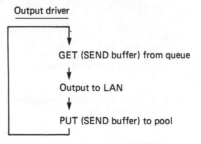

Fig. 7.15 LAN output driver

3. A LAN input driver on the destination computer receives the command. The input driver is more complicated than the output one, but it is also a basic loop (see Fig. 7.16). It gets a RECEIVE buffer from a pool and awaits input from the LAN, signalled by interrupt. It then fills the RECEIVE buffer with the command. One of two main courses can now be followed. Either the command is one of the four basic ones (p-op, v-op, PUT, GET), in which case the driver finds an idle *dummy task*, attaches the RECEIVE buffer to it (e.g. puts a pointer to the buffer in an agreed register), and activates the dummy task. The role of the dummy task in the destination processor is to emulate the calling task in the source processor for the duration of the requested operation. Alternatively the received command is a reply to an operation made by a local task on a remote entity; specifically, a p-operation or a GET. In these cases the input driver reactivates the suspended original task, and (if a GET was called) gives it the data by copying from the RECEIVE buffer into an ordinary buffer, which it gets from a suitable pool, and attaching it to the task. The RECEIVE buffer is returned to the pool.

4. The dummy task is illustrated in Fig. 7.17. There should be as many dummy tasks available per processor as there are possible simultaneous incoming

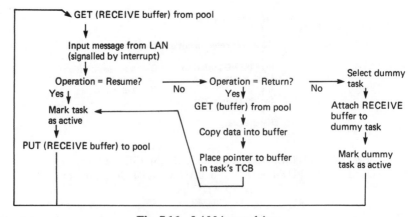

Fig. 7.16 LAN input driver

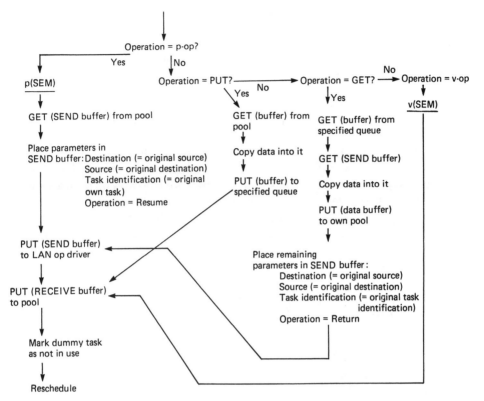

Fig. 7.17   A LAN dummy task to perform calls made from a remote computer

calls from remote tasks. The dummy task has four paths:

p-operation: The normal p(SEM) is called by the dummy task, SEM being now local. When the dummy task continues it gets a SEND buffer, places a Resume command in it, puts it to the LAN output driver for sending back to the original task in the source processor (these details can be found in the RECEIVE buffer which the dummy task still holds), returns the RECEIVE buffer to its pool, and kills itself, thereby freeing the dummy task for future use. What happens when the source processor receives the Resume command has been discussed in 3.

v-operation: The normal v(SEM) is called, SEM being local. The RECEIVE buffer is returned to its pool, and the dummy task freed.

PUT: An ordinary data buffer is got from a suitable pool, the data copied into it from the RECEIVE buffer, it is put to the target queue (local), the RECEIVE buffer is returned to its pool and the dummy task freed.

GET: The normal GET operation is called for the specified queue (local). When a data buffer is acquired it is copied into a got SEND buffer, together with the appropriate Return command. The SEND buffer is put to the LAN output driver, the data and RECEIVE buffers are returned to their pools, the dummy task is freed. What happens when the Source processor receives the Return command has been discussed in 3.

The above mechanisms permit tasks to be distributed over processors on the LANs, yet to intercommunicate as though they were on one processor. The whole distributed program could be written as a unit, with a selective compilation feature causing only the code for a particular processor to be generated for that processor, and also creating the tables defining the location of entities (semaphores, queues).

It will be noticed that there is no provision for handling errors. If the LAN fails to deliver a command, or if a buffer or dummy task is not available in the destination processor, the task in the source processor will carry on regardless or perhaps remain suspended for ever. This defect can easily be remedied at the cost of some more complexity. It is also clear that the Cambridge Ring, with its short minipackets explicitly acknowledged, is more suitable for this kind of use than Ethernet, where short messages imply inefficiency and there is no acknowledgement at all.

References

1. 'Broadband coaxial Local Area Networks', Parts I and II, Mark A. Dineson, *Computer Design*, June and July 1980.

2. 'Ethernet: Distributed Packet Switching for Local Computer Networks', R. M. Metcalfe and D. R. Boggs, *Communications of the ACM*, July 1976, **19**(7).

3. 'The Cambridge Digital Communication Ring', M. V. Wilkes and D. J. Wheeler, *Proceedings of the LACN Symposium*, Mitre and NBS, May 1979.

   A commercial implementation is presented in: *Polynet – Network Manual*, Logica VTS, London, 1981.

4. A commercial implementation of BBP is presented in: *The Basic Block Protocol for Polynet*, Logica VTS, London, 1981.

5. *The Ethernet, A Local Network, Data Link Layer and Physical Layer Specifications.* Digital, Intel, Xerox, September 1980.

Chapter 8   Networks without switching – satellites

Data communication based on a satellite provides another example of a broadcasting system with selective reception. Here we consider only geostationary satellites, which maintain a constant position relative to the earth above the equator, because they circle the earth at the same speed as the earth revolves. Such satellites are really the only feasible candidates for supporting earth-to-earth communications, except for very special applications. This is because they permit 24 h communications between any points covered by the satellite; and because the antennae ('dishes') at those points can have a more or less constant orientation, and need not have expensive systems for tracking the satellite's movement.

Such satellites are of course used for telephony, and data can be sent on any resulting voice channel in the usual manner, and with the usual restrictions – notably speed. However, we are here concerned with high-speed transmission making direct use of the very wide bandwidth supported by satellite transponders, owing to the high-frequency carriers (e.g. 12–14 GHz) they employ. The transponder is an active device on the satellite which receives on one carrier frequency and retransmits on another, and is powered by solar cells. The satellite may carry several transponders, with their antennae designed to receive from and transmit to particular geographical areas beneath the satellite. The bandwidth of a transponder could be, for example 80 MHz which is certainly capable of carrying bit-rates such as 4 Mbps, given a suitable modem.

The attractions of such high-speed transmission are apparent when one considers certain classes of data, in particular digitized 'images' of one form or another. For example, a normal (A4) sheet of paper sampled by a pure black-or-white Group 3 facsimile scanner at, say, 8 samples/mm horizontally and 7.7 lines/mm vertically, gives over 3.8 million samples, or 3.8 Mbits at one bit per sample. This may be reduced considerably (to two or three hundreds of kbits) by compression to eliminate, e.g. white spaces; but could increase equally dramatically if various levels of grey were recognized per sample, or if colour were included, or if the resolution were made finer. Such facsimile documents, in which text and pictures are treated equally by the coding mechanism, require channels of very high bit-rates if they are to be transmitted and received at rates less than 5 s/page, for example.

Given then that we are talking about high-speed transmission via a geostationary satellite, two important characteristics must be taken into account:

1. There is a delay earth-satellite-earth of some 250 ms because the satellite is at an altitude of some 36 000 km, to maintain its geostationary position.

2. The delay means that if the data rate is for example 4 Mbps, there is perhaps 1 Mbit in transit at any time. This has serious consequences for a receiver which encounters any problems, such as running out of buffering space or detecting errors in the received data, since the data in transit cannot be stopped, and much more may be transmitted while the stopping mechanism is operating.

8.1 TDMA for satellites

Although users may wish to have access to a 4 Mbps channel there will be very few who want such access or are prepared to pay for it, even for one hour, let alone 24 hours per day. The volume of traffic per user does not justify it. This leads to the conclusion that, even if the satellite operator is prepared to schedule use of a part of a transponder to different users every hour, many potential users will not find the service cost-effective. The solution is, once again, dynamic TDMA; a dynamic mechanism for allocating users the right to transmit on the high-speed channel.

There are many possible approaches to TDMA for satellites, and two are discussed here. The basic components of such systems are illustrated in Fig. 8.1.

● A computer-like device, with substantial memory, acts as the source and sink of data.

● It is interfaced to an access controller (AC) which determines when the station may transmit, demanding data from the computer accordingly; and which delivers incoming data for that station to the computer. The AC also, probably, has a large memory buffer.

● The AC is connected to further digital equipment such as a scrambler/descrambler and a coder/decoder (codec) for error correction (see later), and thence to the modem.

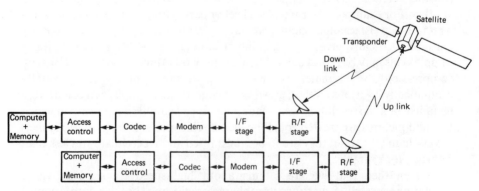

Fig. 8.1 Components of system for data transmission via satellite

- Typical modems for satellites use two- or four-phase shift modulation. Their analogue side is interfaced to the Intermediate Frequency (I/F) stage of the transmitter/receiver.

- The I/F stage is interfaced to the R/F (Radio Frequency) stage which outputs via a power amplifier to a waveguide to the antenna, and which inputs from the waveguide to a low-noise amplifier.

- The antenna itself, a parabolic dish of 2 or 3 m diameter.

We are here concerned with the AC, and how a station determines when it may transmit.

8.1.1 A token-passing access mechanism

The first example of an access control mechanism is that of token-passing. It was originally proposed for the Apollo system for document delivery via the ECS2 satellite. The design has since been modified.

In the Apollo system [1] blocks of data are large, the minimum traffic unit being 480 kbits. Up to ten simultaneously active earth stations are envisaged, and permission to transmit is given to stations by a token-passing procedure based on one for LANs [2] (IEEE 802.4). In this system each station has a number, and a logical ring of stations is formed by considering This Station (TS) as preceded by the station with the next higher number, the Previous Station (PS), and followed by the station with the next lower number, the Next Station (NS). The ring is closed by the highest numbered station following the lowest. A single token is passed round the ring. When TS has finished transmitting data it sends the token to NS. NS either transmits data itself or passes the token at once to its NS; etc. TS knows that the token has been successfully received by NS when it hears NS's transmission. This will be after 2×250 ms $= 0.5$ s plus any response delays in the equipment and software.

Recovery procedures are defined for the cases when TS hears no response from NS, or hears something but it is garbled. If TS eventually decides NS is dead, it can identify the subsequent station by sending a 'who-follows?' message bearing the dead NS's number. The station whose PS number equals this should reply, and the ring is reformed excluding the failed station. TS can also broadcast a more general invitation to respond ('solicit-successor-2') if the ring is broken.

A station can leave the ring implicitly by just failing to take the token, and reconstruction of the ring is as above. A station can also leave explicitly, by sending a special message when it has the token. Stations may enter the ring dynamically. This is done by TS (which could be any station) sending a 'solicit-successor' message every so often, specifying an address range (e.g. between TS and NS). Any would-be entrant with an address within that range should reply, and TS must change its NS address on hearing the reply. Procedures exist for dealing with contention if two would-be entrants reply at once.

As has been stated, the minimum data traffic unit (which may contain data for several destinations) is 480 kbits and the maximum data message should not exceed 20 traffic units, or 9.6 Mbits. Allowing 0.6 s to transfer a token, and 0.25 s per traffic unit at an information rate of 1.92 Mbps, the maximum cycle time for this system (10 stations) is $10 \times (20 \times 0.25 + 0.6) = 56$ s. The efficiency is then also maximum; if we define efficiency as the time used by data ($10 + 20 \times 0.25 = 50$ s) divided by the total time (56 s), efficiency = 89%. At the other extreme, a station wishing to transmit a single traffic unit, when no other stations wish to, could wait up to $10 \times 0.6 = 6$ s and the resulting efficiency would be $100 \times 0.25/6$, or less than 5%.

It is clear that the TDMA scheme described above is suitable for bulk transmission of data where fast response is of little importance.

8.1.2 A centrally controlled access mechanism

A second and very different approach to satellite TDMA is provided by the STELLA, Universe and similar projects [3]. Here the 250 ms loop-delay time is not wasted, as it is in the previous scheme. Instead, one or more new stations may start transmitting more or less immediately after the previous senders' messages have been sent but before they have been received (see Fig. 8.2.).

The scheme is based on a Frame whose beginning is determined by a Reference Burst emitted by a Master Station. The Reference Burst arrives at all stations (including the Master) 'simultaneously' some 250 ms after transmission. It defines a starting-point in time. Each station in the system is allocated a very short slot near the beginning of the frame, in which it may transmit a request for time in a subsequent frame in which it may transmit *data*. For example, in Fig. 8.2 the frame time is slightly longer than half the 250 ms loop delay, so that A's request for time can be acknowledged (with a time allocation) by the Master two frames later. The allocation will give a starting time and a duration for A's data burst within the frame, and be coded in the Master's Reference Burst. The Reference Burst with the allocation will reach A 250 ms later, thereby authorizing A actually to transmit in the fourth frame after his original request.

Because of variations between stations in the 'simultaneity' of reception of

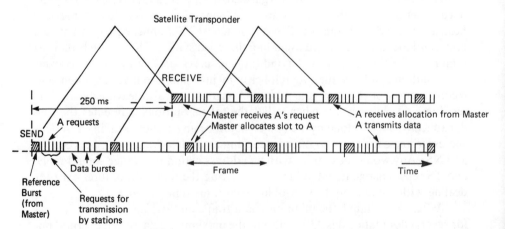

Fig. 8.2   A TDMA scheme for a satellite link

the Reference Burst (due among other things to drifting of the satellite), there must be 'guard slots' of silence between the times of transmission of different stations within the frame. A guard slot of 1 ms corresponds to a difference in the length of the paths from the Master to two other stations of ± 150 km.

In this tightly synchronized use of the frame various problems arise. Short bursts may imply an overhead of time lost in the modem while it locks into a new burst. Error detection and error correction procedures may also imply an overhead in the form of preambles to each burst (see below). If a transparency procedure, such as HDLC's bit-stuffing, is employed the size of a burst is known only approximately by the AC, and larger guard slots must be allocated. Nevertheless, if we suppose the system supports 10 stations, that the reference burst is 5 ms, the request bursts 1 ms, up to three data bursts per frame are allowed, the guard slot is 1 ms, and the frame length 130 ms, then the efficiency could be $(130 - (5 + 10 \times 1 + 10 \times 1 + 3 \times 1))/130$ or 77%. The response delay obviously depends on the Master's allocation algorithm, but usually there are not more than five frames between requesting a time-slot and actually transmitting data in it, i.e. less than 0.7 s. This TDMA scheme is obviously well suited to relatively short bursts of data, such as 30 ms or 60 kbits at 2 Mbps, where fast response is important.

8.2 Error correction on reception

What happens if there are errors on a satellite link? In fact BERs of 10^{-6} are to be expected, which at Mbit rates means one error or more per second. Error correction by requesting retransmission is hardly feasible because of the quantity of data in transit and the large loop delay; not to mention the problems which arise if broadcasting to many receivers, some of which may experience an error while others do not. The solution to the problem is forward error correction, or error correction (as well as detection) on *reception*.

The general concept of error correction is as follows. The valid messages (codewords) form a subset of all possible messages, essentially because valid messages are composed of arbitrary data bits supplemented by check digits which are not arbitrary, but are dependent on the data bits. Thus if transmission is in the form of blocks of n bits, of which k bits are arbitrary data, the remaining $(n - k)$ bits are determined completely by the k data bits. Of the 2^n possible vectors (i.e. strings of n bits) only 2^k are valid codewords or code vectors. The error-correcting procedure on reception is therefore to attempt to find the codeword which is closest to the actual received vector (block); that is, which differs from it in the least number of bits. The number of differing bits is termed the 'Hamming distance' between two vectors. The received block is assumed to be a corruption of the codeword at least distance from it, and is replaced by it – thus correcting, hopefully, the errors.

It is clear that if the minimum distance between any pair of codewords is d_{min}, then in principle it is possible to *detect* any error pattern of m bits $(m < d_{min})$; and to correct any error pattern of t bits $(t \leqslant (d_{min} - 1)/2)$ since the erroneous vector will lie nearer one codeword than any other. The art of designing error-correcting codes and procedures is thus two-fold:

1. How to design a coding procedure which will create a set of codewords with a large d_{min} for a small value of $(n - k)$; to maximize the error-correcting possibilities and to minimize the number of check digits. (Note: this goal is suitable for correcting *random* errors. Codes for correcting bursts of errors also exist, but are not discussed here.)

2. How to design a decoding, i.e. error-correcting, procedure which will match a received vector with the nearest valid codeword; and which is quicker than doing an exhaustive search through all possible codewords.

We discuss here two approaches, majority logic decodable (MLD) codes and convolutional codes, which are both used on satellite links. The discussion is necessarily somewhat superficial, but, it is hoped, useful.

8.2.1 Majority Logic Decodable codes

MLD codes [4] are a special class of cyclic codes which in turn are a special class of linear block codes. An (n, k) linear block code is a k-dimensional vector space composed of n-tuples. In simpler language the code consists of vectors of n bits, but any codeword can be expressed as a linear combination of at most k basic codewords. 'Combining' consists of XORing corresponding bits in two vectors. It can be shown that a linear code can be put in systematic form

$$\mathbf{c} = \mathbf{mG}$$

where $\mathbf{c}$ is the resulting codeword (n bits), $\mathbf{m}$ is a vector of k arbitrary message (data) bits, and $\mathbf{G}$ is the $k \times n$ generator matrix

$$\mathbf{G} = \begin{matrix} p_{11} & p_{12} & \cdots & p_{1(n-k)} & 1 & 0 & 0 & \cdots & 0 \\ p_{21} & \vdots & & \vdots & 0 & 1 & 0 & \cdots & 0 \\ \vdots & \ddots \vdots & & \vdots & & \vdots & \vdots & \vdots & \vdots \\ p_{k1} & p_{k2} & \cdots & p_{k(n-k)} & 0 & 0 & 0 & \cdots & 1 \end{matrix}$$

It is clear that $\mathbf{c} = (c_1, c_2 \cdots c_{n-k}, m_1, m_2 \cdots m_k)$ with

$$c_i = \sum_{1 \leqslant j \leqslant k} m_j p_{ji} \qquad (1 \leqslant i \leqslant n - k)$$

so that the codeword consists of the data bits plus check digits formed from the data bits.

By inspection it can be shown that $\mathbf{cH}^T = 0$, for any codeword $\mathbf{c}$, where $\mathbf{H}^T$ is the transpose of the $(n - k) \times n$ matrix

$$\mathbf{H} = \begin{matrix} 1 & 0 & 0 & \cdots & 0 & p_{11} & & \cdots & p_{k1} \\ 0 & 1 & & \cdots & 0 & \vdots & & & \vdots \\ \vdots & \vdots & & & \vdots & \vdots & & & \vdots \\ 0 & 0 & & \cdots & 1 & p_{1(n-k)} & & \cdots & p_{k(n-k)} \end{matrix}$$

Thus if $\mathbf{r}$ is a received vector and $\mathbf{e}$ an error vector added to $\mathbf{c}$ during transmission, $\mathbf{r} = \mathbf{c} + \mathbf{e}$, we can define a vector of $(n - k)$ bits, the *syndrome*, $\mathbf{s}$, with

$$\mathbf{s} = \mathbf{r}\mathbf{H}^{\mathrm{T}} = (\mathbf{c} + \mathbf{e})\mathbf{H}^{\mathrm{T}} = 0 + \mathbf{e}\mathbf{H}^{\mathrm{T}} = \mathbf{e}\mathbf{H}^{\mathrm{T}}$$

where $\mathbf{H}^{\mathrm{T}}$ is the transpose of $\mathbf{H}$. In other words if on reception we calculate the syndrome $\mathbf{r}\mathbf{H}^{\mathrm{T}}$, we get information about the errors since $\mathbf{s} = \mathbf{e}\mathbf{H}^{\mathrm{T}}$. Maybe from $\mathbf{s}$ we can infer $\mathbf{e}$ and so recreate $\mathbf{c} = \mathbf{r} + \mathbf{e}$ (remembering $+ = -$ in XOR arithmetic).

In fact it is obvious that, for single error patterns $\mathbf{e} = (0 \ldots 010 \ldots 0)$ where the 1 is in the ith bit position, $\mathbf{s}$ is the ith row of $\mathbf{H}^{\mathrm{T}}$. Conversely if all rows of $\mathbf{H}^{\mathrm{T}}$ are distinct, then if $\mathbf{s}$ is found to equal the ith row we may infer the error pattern is $(0 \ldots 010 \ldots 0)$ with 1 in the ith bit position. All rows of $\mathbf{H}^{\mathrm{T}}$ are easily made distinct if the number of possible non-zero bit patterns left to make up the rows of p_{ij} terms $(2^{n-k} - (n - k) - 1)$ is greater than or equal to the number of actual rows, k. In short, the single-error correcting procedure described will work if

$$2^{n-k} - (n - k) - 1 \geqslant k$$

or
$$2^{n-k} \geqslant n + 1$$

or
$$n - k \geqslant \log_2 (n + 1)$$

The reader may verify the above statements by considering the $(7, 4)$ linear code whose generator matrix

$$\mathbf{G} = \begin{array}{ccccccc} 1 & 1 & 1 & 1 & 0 & 0 & 0 \\ 1 & 1 & 0 & 0 & 1 & 0 & 0 \\ 1 & 0 & 1 & 0 & 0 & 1 & 0 \\ 0 & 1 & 1 & 0 & 0 & 0 & 1 \end{array}$$

The valid codewords in this code are:

0 0 0 0 0 0 0	1 1 0 0 1 0 0	1 1 1 1 0 0 0	0 0 1 1 1 0 0
0 1 1 0 0 0 1	1 0 1 0 1 0 1	1 0 0 1 0 0 1	0 1 0 1 1 0 1
1 0 1 0 0 1 0	0 1 1 0 1 1 0	0 1 0 1 0 1 0	1 0 0 1 1 1 0
1 1 0 0 0 1 1	0 0 0 0 1 1 1	0 0 1 1 0 1 1	1 1 1 1 1 1 1

It will be seen that for this code $d_{\min} = 3$, so single bit errors are always correctable. Another way of seeing this is to note that no codeword (except the zero codeword) has less than three non-zero bits; therefore $d_{\min} = 3$, since it is a linear code and if the distance between some pair c_1 and c_2 were less than 3, there would exist a codeword $c = c_1 + c_2$ with less than three non-zero bits.

In practice we are concerned with much more powerful codes than simple single-error correcting linear codes. A powerful subclass of linear codes is that of cyclic codes. A cyclic code is a linear code in which if $\mathbf{c}$ is a codeword then $\mathbf{c}^{(1)}$, namely $\mathbf{c}$ rotated right one bit, is also a codeword. Using the polynomial representation of an earlier chapter, we can represent $c = (c_0 \ldots c_{n-1})$ by

$$c = c_{n-1} + c_{n-2}x + \cdots + c_1 x^{n-2} + c_0 x^{n-1}$$

It is easily seen that

$$c^{(1)} = c_0 + c_{n-1}x + c_{n-2}x + \cdots + c_e x^{n-2} + c_1 x^{n-1}$$

$$= xc + c_0(1 + x^n)$$

In general

$$c^{(i)} = x^i c + (1 + x^n)(c_0 x^{i-1} + c_1 x^{i-2} + \cdots + c_{i-2}x + c_{i-1}) \tag{8.1}$$

A cyclic code can be generated from a generating polynomial $G(x)$. On the one hand, given a cyclic code, one can find the highest common factor polynomial of all the code vectors, $G(x)$. A little consideration will show that it too is a code vector, so all products $Q(x) G(x)$ of degree less than n must also be code vectors. $G(x)$ must be of degree $(n - k)$ itself, and it must divide $(1 + x^n)$, see Equation 8.1 above. Conversely, if $G(x)$ of degree $(n - k)$ divides $(1 + x^n)$, it generates a cyclic code whose codewords are $Q(x) G(x)$ where $Q(x)$ is an arbitrary polynomial of degree $(k - 1)$. Such a code is not in systematic form. A cyclic code can be put in systematic form by defining

$$c(x) = r(x) + x^{n-k}m(x) \tag{8.2}$$

where $m(x)$ is the message, and $r(x)$ is the remainder on dividing $x^{n-k}m(x)$ by $G(x)$

$$r(x) + G(x)b(x) = x^{n-k}m(x) \tag{8.3}$$

Combining Equations 8.2 and 8.3 we see $c(x)$ is divisible by $G(x)$.

The generator matrix of such a code has its p_{ij} formed as follows:

$$P_i(x) = p_{i1} + p_{i2}x + \cdots + p_{i(n-k)}x^{n-k-1}$$

$$= \text{Remainder on dividing } x^{n-k-1+i} \text{ by } G(x)$$

As a result, if $E_{n-1}(x) = e_{n-1} + \cdots + e_1 x^{n-2} + e_0 x^{n-1}$ is an error polynomial, its syndrome s, as previously defined, is

$$(s_0\ s_1 \ldots s_{n-k-1}) = (e_{n-1}, e_{n-2}, \ldots, e_0)H^{\mathrm{T}}$$

or

$$S(x) = s_0 + s_1 x + \cdots + s_{n-k-1}x^{n-k-1}$$

$$= e_{n-1} + e_{n-2}x + \cdots + e_k x^{n-k-1} + e_{k-1}P_1(x)$$

$$+ e_{k-2}P_2(x) + \cdots + e_0 P_k(x)$$

$$= e_{n-1} + e_{n-2}x + \cdots + e_k x^{n-k-1} + e_{k-1}(x^{n-k} + B_{n-k}G)$$

$$+ e_0(x^{n-1} + B_{n-1}G)$$

$$= E_n(x) + BG(x)$$

Thus the syndrome is the remainder on dividing the error polynomial by $G(x)$. (The $B(x)$ polynomials are of no interest.)

Returning to the original two points (how to design codes with large $d_{\min}$ and small $(n - k)$, and how to find simple error-correcting procedures for them) we have made the following progress:

- Cyclic codes can be constructed to have large d_{min}, small $(n - k)$. This is essentially because all codewords are products of $G(x)$. The coefficients of the powers of x in $G(x)$ are combinations of the values of the roots of $G(x)$, which are a subset of the roots of $1 + x^n$, and therefore the coefficients of the powers of x in all codewords are also combinations of these roots. A large d_{min} requires (see above) that all non-zero code vectors have many non-zero coefficients; and this can be forced to occur if the roots are suitably chosen to be refractory to combinations which result in zeros, i.e. zero coefficients. (Analogy: no rational combination of $\sqrt{2}$ and $\sqrt{3}$ can be made to vanish.)
- The syndrome calculated from a received vector in a linear code gives information as to the error. With cyclic codes the syndrome is the remainder on division by the generating polynomial. In Chapter 3 we have seen that this remainder is easily calculated with a feedback shift register.

We do not elaborate further on the design of these cyclic codes, but proceed to explain how, given the syndrome of a received rector, it can be used to correct that received vector.

Figure 8.3 illustrates a scheme for error correction using the syndrome of the received vector. Firstly, with switches S_{IN} closed, S_{OUT} open, the syndrome is calculated as we have seen in a previous chapter. The syndrome, S_0, is in fact the remainder on dividing $x^{n-k}E_n(s)$ by $G(x)$, since the transmitted codeword itself is divisible by $G(x)$. Here we define $E_n(x)$ as

$$E_n(x) = e_0 x^{n-1} + e_1 x^{n-2} + \cdots + e_{n-1}$$

The scheme is designed to correct 'correctable' errors. A correctable error sequence is one in which the received vector is nearer to the transmitted codeword than to any other codeword. Each correctable error sequence will have an associated syndrome. Obviously if distinct errors give rise to distinct syndromes the decoder, whose function it is to determine the error sequence, is straightforward – as we have seen before.

The decoder in Fig. 8.3 is designed to handle this case, but rather than reconstructing all $E_n(x)$ at once it only calculates the right-hand bit, e_0. Its

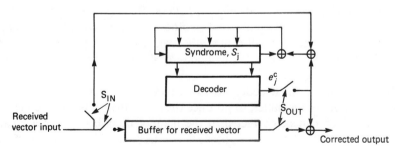

Fig. 8.3 Decoder and correction for MLD codes

function is therefore to reconstruct the most right-hand bit of the correctable error sequences which could have given rise to the syndromes it is supplied with.

From Fig. 8.3 it can also be seen that as S_0 is calculated by shifting in the received vector, so the received vector is also buffered in an n-bit register. Error correction proceeds by opening the S_{IN}, closing the S_{OUT} switches and shifting the syndrome and buffer registers right. The output of the decoder each time is XORed with the syndrome's right-hand bit and fed back, and also XORed with the received vector's right-hand bit.

We call the decoder's output $e_0^c, e_1^c, \ldots, e_{i-1}^c$ after i shifts, where e_j^c is the most right-hand bit of the correctable error pattern giving rise to syndrome S_j of the sequence $S_0, S_1, \ldots, S_j, \ldots, S_{i-1}$. Then, as we have seen previously,

$$S_i(x) = x^i S_0(x) + C_i(x)G(x) + x^{n-k}E_i^c(x)$$

with

$$E_i^c(x) = e_0^c x^{i-1} + e_1^c x^{i-2} + \cdots + e_{i-1}^c$$

so

$$S_i(x) = x^i(B_n(x)G(x) + x^{n-k}E_n(x)) + C_i(x)G(x) + x^{n-k}E_i^c(x)$$
$$= D_i(x)G(x) + x^{n-k}(x^i E_n(x) + E_i^c(x))$$
$$= D_i(x)G(x) + x^{n-k}(x^i(E_n(x) + x^{n-i}E_i^c(x)) + E_i^c(x)(1 + x^n))$$

or

$$S_i(x) = P_i(x)G(x) + x^{n-k}x^i(E_n(x) + x^{n-i}E_i^c(x)) \qquad (8.4)$$

Since $(1 + x^n)$ is divisible by $G(x)$, $(C_i, B_n, D_i, P_i$ are quotient polynomials of no interest).

Equation 8.4 states that $S_i(x)$ is the remainder on dividing $x^{16}x^i(E_n(x) + x^{n-i}E_i^c(x))$ by $G(x)$ taking $n - k = 16$, as applies, for example, in HDLC.

If we suppose that the decoder's output determines the actual errors e_j, $0 \leqslant j \leqslant i - 1$, so that $e_j = e_j^c$ and the actual errors were correctable errors; then $S(x)$ is the remainder on dividing $x^{16}(e_i x^{n-1} + e_{i+1}x^{n-2} + \cdots + e_{n-1}x^i + 0 + 0 + \cdots + 0)$ by $G(x)$. But if the original $E_n(x)$ was a correctable error sequence so is this new dividend, which is $E_n(x)$ shifted right i bits and truncated. Thus, by hypothesis, e_i^c will equal e_i; etc. In other words, and by induction, if $E_n(x)$ is correctable, the decoder will generate a sequence $e_j^c = e_j$ $0 \leqslant j \leqslant n - 1$. The final value of the syndrome, $S_n(x)$, will be zero; if it is not, then $E_n(x)$ was not a correctable error sequence.

It is clear that if the decoder works correctly, it also corrects the received vector shifted out of the buffer, to produce the originally transmitted codeword.

Codes which can be corrected in the manner described above are called Majority Logic Decodable codes, because the decoder which produces e_j^c from $S_j(x)$ can be built with simple majority logic.

8.2.2 Error correction – convolutional codes

The problem with the MLD procedure just illustrated is that the received vector is buffered and then corrected. On satellite links, where blocks are long, a large buffer is required. Additionally if there is not an adequate pause between blocks while correction takes place, some sort of double-buffering technique is required so that correction of one block can take place while the next is being received. MLD procedures are thus suitable for short burst transmissions as in the second example of satellite TDM given above, using the synchronized frame.

With longer transmission bursts convolutional coding, which does not require a large buffer, is preferable.

In convolutional coding redundant bits are inserted into the data stream continuously. The message itself may remain intact, with, for example, a check bit added after every two message bits, giving a two-thirds rate code. Alternatively, the message also may be changed. In the convolutional coder illustrated in Fig. 8.4 two bits are sent for every message bit. In general b bits ($b = 1$ in our example) are shifted at a time into a k-stage ($k = 4$) shift register, to which are attached n ($n = 2$) combinatorial circuits. The coder's output is a cyclic sample of the outputs of each of these circuits, at every time slot. In the example two bits are sent for every one bit input to the coder, so the rate is one half.

There are many types of convolutional codes, and many ways of designing decoding strategies and circuits. Here we shall not go into details, the subject being more of an art than a science in any case, but rather present two aspects:

- how to analyse the properties of a given code, in particular the distance between codewords, for the correction of random errors;
- an algorithm for the decoding of a received vector which gives the most likely codeword that, when corrupted, could have given rise to the received vector (maximum likelihood decoding).

The presentation draws heavily on Viterbi's paper [5].

The behaviour of a convolutional coder can be represented by a state diagram. Figure 8.5 is the state diagram for the coder of Fig. 8.4. There are 2^{k-1} ($= 8$) states, corresponding to all possible values of the most significant ($k - 1$) bits in the register. The least significant bit determines the n-bit (2-bit) symbol emitted on transition to the next state, when the register is shifted left. The states are named a ($= 000$), b ($= 001$) to h ($= 111$) in Fig. 8.5 and the symbols emitted are placed beside the arrows representing the transitions. Also in the diagram

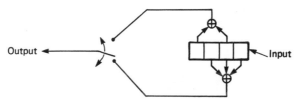

Fig. 8.4 A convolutional encoder

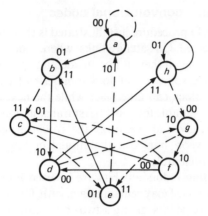

Fig. 8.5   State diagram of code of Fig. 8.4

those transitions corresponding to an input 1 are marked with a solid line, those corresponding to a 0 with a dashed line.

As with all codes, in convolutional codes the 2^m valid codewords (corresponding to all possible inputs of m-bits to the coder) form a subset of all the possible vectors of (m/R) bits, where R is the code rate. The minimum distance, d_{min}, between any pair of codewords defines the detection and correction capabilities of the code. It is easily shown that the valid codewords form a 'group' – i.e. the (XOR) sum of any two codewords is itself a codeword, there is a zero codeword, and every codeword has an inverse (itself). This being so, there is no loss of generality in considering the distances between the zero codeword and all other codewords, as opposed to considering the distances between some non-zero and all other codewords.

Figure 8.6 is Fig. 8.5 redrawn. It shows on each transition between states, the distance between the symbol emitted and the 00 symbol, as a power i ($i = 0, 1, 2$) of D, an operator. The node a has also been split open. It represents the path of the all-zero codewords. Other codewords deviate from it, by following the arrows

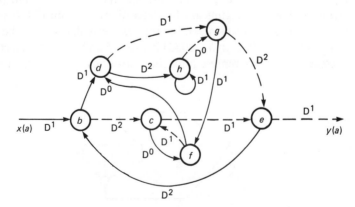

Fig. 8.6   Distances between emitted symbols and 00

round the diagram until, eventually, they return to a. We define two other operators, L and N, where the powers of L indicate the number of transitions we have passed through, and the powers of N give the number of non-zero inputs which occurred (giving rise to continuous arrows), when following arrows round the diagram.

We may now write equations such as:

$$h = LDNh + LD^2Nd$$

This says that the powers of D, L, N characterizing a path which has reached state h may be calculated by multiplying this same state of the path at h by LDN (one transition, distance from 00 is 1, continuous line) and adding (OR) the 'state of the path at d' multiplied by LD^2N. Calling the exit from a state x, and the return to a state y, we can write the following equations:

$$b = LNDx + LND^2e$$

$$c = LD^2b + LDf$$

$$d = LDNb + LNf$$

$$e = LDc + LD^2g$$

$$f = LNc + LDNg$$

$$g = Lh + LDd$$

$$h = LDNh + LDNd$$

$$y = LDe$$

These may be solved for y in terms of x:

$$y = L^4ND^5x/(1 - (LN + L^2N) - L^3ND^5)$$
$$= (L^4ND^5 + (L^5 + L^6)N^2D^6 + (L^6 + 2L^7 + L^8)N^3D^7 + \cdots)x$$

$$(8.5)$$

This states that the nearest codeword (which has returned to state a) to the all zero codeword is at distance 5 from it, passes through four transitions outside the a state, and involves one non-zero input bit. The next near codewords are of distance 6; there are two of them, one involving 5, the other 6, 'non-a' transitions; and they correspond to two non-zero input bits.

Many conclusions can be drawn from Equation 8.5. For example, assuming all codewords end at a ($(k - 1)$ zeros at the end of the input stream will ensure this) then $d_{min} = 5$, so any transmission error affecting two or fewer bits can be corrected, since the received vector is nearer the corrupted codeword than any other. Again, if there are 5 bits in error which have corrupted one codeword into another, then we shall conclude that the original input was different from the real input by only one bit ($N = 1$).

We define the 'first-event error' as having occurred when we first return to state a having wandered away from it. In other words, a first-event error occurs when all-zeros are transmitted, but due to corruption of the transmitted codeword we have concluded that some non-zero codeword was sent, but ending at a. We can calculate an upper bound for the probability of a first event error, P_E, by putting $N = 1, L = 1$ in Equation 8.1, and substituting P_k for D^k. Here P_k is the probability of picking the non-zero codewords of distance k from the all-zero codewords. It is easily seen, by considering the number of ways half or more of the required k bits may be corrupted, that when k is odd

$$P_k = \sum_{j=(k+1/2)}^{k} \frac{k!}{(k-j)!\,j!}\, p^j(1-p)^{k-j}$$

and when k is even

$$P_k = \sum_{j=(k/2)+1}^{k} \frac{k!}{(k-j)!\,j!}\, p^j(1-p)^{k-j} + \frac{1}{2}\frac{k!}{(k/2)!^2}\, p^{k/2}(1-p)^{k/2}$$

where p is the probability of corruption of a single bit. In our case

$$P_E < P_5 + 2P_6 + 4P_7 \cdots$$

It is an upper bound, i.e. an inequality, because the probabilities of decoding incorrectly are not disjoint.

It is possible also to get an upper bound for the bit error rate after correction (CBER). This is in fact the estimated number of input bits which will be wrongly reconstructed. The powers of N in Equation 8.5 give the number of input bits involved for each possible distance, so, using the probabilities as weights,

$$\text{CBER} < P_5 + 2.2P_6 + 3.4P_7 + \cdots$$

For a raw bit error rate of $p = 2 \times 10^{-4}$ on the channel, numerical evaluation gives

$$\text{CBER} < 4 \times 10^{-10}$$

It has been assumed that the decoding procedure consists in considering the received vector and finding the valid codeword nearest to it. This can be done 'on the fly' using Viterbi's algorithm, rather than awaiting the arrival of the complete vector. The procedure uses the state diagram (Fig. 8.5). At each step we could be in any one of the 2^{k-1} (8) states. Assume we can associate with each state two items:

1. A 'survivor' path through the previous states which could have led us to this state. The survivor is that path whose associated generated symbols are at least distance from the received vector. The path can be characterized by the states passed through, e.g. ... *bdhhgf*... , or more usefully by the input sequence giving rise to these states (as determined from the continuous or dashed transitions).

2. The accumulated distance to the received vector associated with that path.

The algorithm proceeds as follows. A new n-bit (2-bit) symbol arrives. We consider the eight possible new states one by one. Each state can be reached by only 2^b (2) paths, one from each of two previous states. We calculate the distance between the received symbol and the symbol theoretically emitted on transition from such a previous state, and add to it the accumulated distance (item 2) associated with that previous state. Comparing the new accumulated distances for the two paths to the state we are considering, we choose that path which has less distance to be the new survivor. For example if we are considering state a, and the new received symbol is 11, this is at distance 2 from a transition from a, and distance 1 from a transition from e. If the accumulated distances for the survivor paths for a and e were previously equal, we choose the one from e to be the new survivor.

Implementing the algorithm involves solving two practical problems:

- How to memorize 2^{k-1} paths without using excessive storage? Fortunately it can be shown that paths can be truncated M steps, say, back from the present. As we add on a new state (input bit) at the head of each path, we save a single bit M steps back in a unique register holding the reconstructed input. The value of that bit is that of the bit that will be truncated from the current optimum (least distance out of 2^{k-1}) path. If M is large compared with k the errors introduced by truncation are small.

- How to synchronize coder and decoder? It is necessary for the decoder to know which of the n bits in the received symbols is the first. One method of synchronization is to send a preamble to the data. For example, in our case, continuous 1s input will result in repeated 01 (state h) on output; and the decoder can be primed to know that this will occur and that 0 is the first bit of the symbol. Alternatively trial and error can be used, the decoder assuming it has wrong synchronization if all path distances are large and approximately equal.

As has been stated, many types of convolutional codes exist and the above discussion is only an introduction. Their great attraction for satellite transmission is that powerful correction of errors can be effected as the bits arrive, thereby saving buffers and time. They are also employed on terrestrial links; for example in the new full duplex 9600 bps V32 modem for use on the public switched telephone network.

8.3 Encryption

Data sent via satellite are broadcast to earth again, and any person with suitable equipment can receive them. An unauthorized receiver can also operate with very little risk of detection, since he requires no physical connection to any network. Authorized users may wish to inhibit unauthorized reception of information for which they are paying, or which is confidential, by encrypting the data sent. (Encryption is of course of potential interest in all forms of data communication, not merely via satellite [6].)

Figure 8.7 illustrates the basic encryption process. The sender uses a *key* to modify the data he wishes to send in the encryptor. A very simple encryptor could perform an XOR between the key and the data (considered as binary strings) and

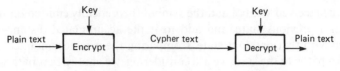

Fig. 8.7 The encryption/decryption procedure

transmit the result. On reception, the same key is applied to the received stream in the decryptor and the original data are recovered. In certain cases users may wish to encrypt not only their data, but also all header and similar information, e.g. destination station address. In this way an outsider is kept ignorant not only of the data but also of the traffic, or how much is being sent to whom. If encrypted bogus traffic is always sent when there is no real traffic, it becomes impossible for an outsider to estimate even total real traffic.

A simple XOR encryptor is easily 'attacked' if an outsider can get hold of some known *plain text* (unencrypted data) and its encrypted form. He can readily determine the key by XORing them together. This 'known plain text attack' can be applied with other encryption mechanisms, and the authorized user should take care to ensure that plain text is not available to outsiders, and cannot be guessed. For example, an outsider could guess the contents of encrypted headers, unless they are systematically altered by adding serial numbers, the time and date, etc. (Another approach is to arrange for known plain text to be introduced, the so-called 'chosen plain text' attack.)

In traditional cryptography both the keys and the encrypting algorithms were kept secret. However, as encryption has become more widespread, largely for commercial rather than the traditional military reasons, it has been recognized that there are advantages in not having secret algorithms. On the contrary, a standard algorithm can be more widely used, enabling the encryptor/decryptor device to be manufactured more cheaply. Secrecy is only required for the keys, and any persons wishing to communicate using the standard encryption process must first agree on a common key or set of keys.

8.3.1 The Data Encryption Standard

A well known algorithm, specifically designed for data transmission, is the Data Encryption Standard (DES) [7] of the US National Bureau of Standards. It operates on blocks of 64 bits at a time, and is illustrated schematically in Fig. 8.8. The algorithm is approximately as follows:

1. The 64 bits are permuted and then split into two 32-bit sets, known as Left (L_1) and Right (R_1).
2. L_1 is passed through a function F, where it is transformed by a key K_1, to produce an output $X_1 = F(L_1, K_1)$.
3. The output is XORed with R_1 to produce an output $R_2 = X_1 + R_1$.
4. The roles of L and R are now reversed. R_2 is put through F, transformed by a new key K_2, to produce an output X_2 which is XORed with L_1 to produce $L_2 = X_2 + L_1$.

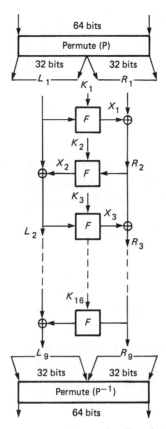

Fig. 8.8   Data Encryption Standard (DES)

5. The process repeats until 16 passes through F have occurred, i.e. 16 keys used. Figure 8.9 illustrates how this may be done by repeated use of the same functional elements.

6. The final output (L_9, R_9) is subjected to the reverse permutation of step 1, and then recombined to form the full 64 bits encrypted.

Consideration of Fig. 8.8 shows that encrypted 64 bits, put through the procedure backwards, are decrypted. Thus an input R_9 produces X_{16}, which XORed with

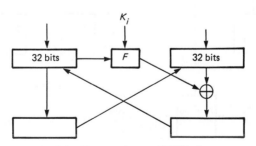

Fig. 8.9   Repeated use of DES elements

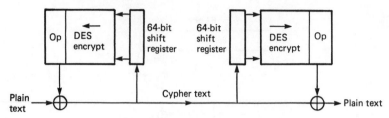

Fig. 8.10 Stream encryption using DES

L_9 produces L_8, etc; with L_1, R_1 finally emerging at the top; provided the keys are applied in the reverse order also. The keys themselves are 48 bits in length and the 32-bit input to F is expanded to 48 bits for merging with the key. The schedule of 16 keys is itself generated from a basic 64-bit input of which 56 bits are used. The complete encryptor, decryptor and key generation functions are available in the form of integrated circuits.

The DES algorithm can be made to operate on a continuous stream (see Fig. 8.10) of bits, by using it to generate a feedback stream, delayed one bit, to modify the data by XORing. Decrypting is the reverse process.

(Note: DES is subject to licensing agreements.)

8.3.2 Encryption on satellite links in practice

Figure 8.11 illustrates an encryption system applied by British Telecom to its SatStream service [8], running at 2.048 Mbit/s. Data are carried in PCM-like frames of 64 8-bit slots, four slots of which are used for control purposes. The 'cryptographic engine' of Fig. 8.11 does not use DES, but TACA, an algorithm based on 96-bit keys. It uses not only keys, but also an initial *input vector* (IV), which is transmitted by the sender in the control octets of the frame. The output of

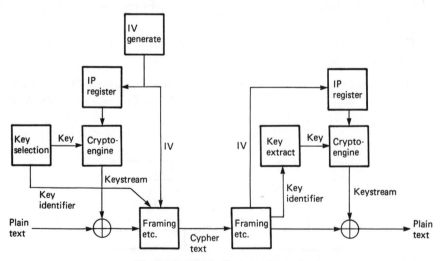

Fig. 8.11 BT SatStream encryption

the encryption engine, which is XORed with the plain text, is known as the *keystream*. The keystream must obviously be correctly synchronized with the cipher text on reception to decrypt, and this is achieved by using the framing and IV information.

Keys are distributed physically in a secure box called a *key gun*, which can be plugged into the central key generating unit to load the keys, and then later plugged into the encryption engines for unloading and use. The control octets in the transmitted frame indicate which key is to be used and the keys are sequentially extracted by the engine, at a rate, say, of once per day.

The system is relatively simple and is suitable to the situation where potential receivers are divided into two classes: authorized and unauthorized. In the TDMA scheme discussed in Section 8.1.1, a more complex situation prevails. The authorized receivers are not necessarily all simultaneously authorized to receive the same data. The transmitter should have private sets of keys for each authorized receiver, as well as sets of keys for broadcasting to all members of groups. If traffic patterns, as well as data, are to be secret, then perhaps the token-passing mechanism itself should be encrypted. The secure management, identification and distribution of keys is clearly a problematic area [6].

8.3.3 Public key systems

A possible solution to the problem of key distribution is provided by the well known *public key* approach of Diffie and Hellman [9], and its 'implementation' by Rivest, Shamir and Adleman (RSA) [10]. Although the RSA method can be used for encrypting all the data, the computing time involved in performing the necessary mathematics is normally unacceptable. Thus we shall suppose that the method is used only to distribute keys of a more conventional algorithm such as DES or TACA.

In public key systems a user has a mechanism for generating *two* keys; one public, one secret. Any message, K, encrypted using the public key produces a cipher text $E_p(K)$. This can only be decrypted using the secret key: *the public key will not decrypt it*. If we represent decryption by the operation D_s, then

$$K = D_s(E_p(K)) \tag{8.6}$$

In our satellite example K could be the conventional key for a receiver, which has to be distributed to him from a key management centre, for example via satellite. To do this a user, A, sends by any (insecure) means, his public key (P_A) to the centre. When the centre wishes to give that user a new conventional key, K_A, he sends him $E_{P_A}(K_A)$. The user applies D_{S_A}, where S_A is the secret key, to reconstruct K_A for future use on data. The fact that P_A could be intercepted and stolen is of no worry, unless the thief somehow manages to use it to send the user a fraudulent conventional key, K_F. But even this can be prevented, as follows:

In the RSA system the operators D_s and E_p commute, so that

$$K = E_p(D_s(K)) \tag{8.7}$$

Equation 8.7 permits authentication of messages. Suppose the centre has public key P_c and secret key S_c. Then using Equation 8.7 the centre can send an encrypted message $D_{S_c}(K)$ which all holders of P_c can decrypt – *but no-one other than the centre could have created it*. Indeed the receiver himself could not have forged it, since he does not know S_c.

This attribute can be used to ensure that false conventional keys, K_F, cannot be sent. For example, the centre could send a message M containing the new conventional key, K_A, and some legible text such as the centre's identity, the date and time, and the user's identity, A.

$$M = \text{Text} + K_A$$

The centre then encrypts this, using S_c, to produce $D_{S_c}(M)$. He further encrypts this using E_{P_A} to produce

$$E_{P_A}(D_{S_c}(M))$$

This transmitted message can only be read by the holder of S_A, by performing D_{S_A}: and when he then performs E_{P_c} to recover M he is also sure that the key received, K_A, is genuine if the text is what he expects.

It remains to explain how the operations E and D function, and how keys are generated in the RSA case.

E and D consist in raising integers (i.e. a string of binary bits representing a message, but considered as an integer) to powers, modulo-N. (Modulo-N of a number is the remainder on dividing by N.)

$$E_p(K) = K^p \quad (\text{modulo-}N)$$

$$D_s(K) = K^s \quad (\text{modulo-}N)$$

So for Equations 8.6 and 8.7 to hold we require, for all K,

$$K = K^{ps} \quad (\text{modulo-}N) \tag{8.8}$$

The method of determining p, s and N so that Equation 8.8 holds is as follows:

1. Choose two prime numbers x, y. Then $N = xy$.
2. Choose p such that the greatest common divider of p and $(x - 1)(y - 1)$ is 1, i.e. p is prime to $(x - 1)$ and $(y - 1)$.
3. Find s such that $ps = 1$ (modulo $(x - 1)(y - 1)$). This can always be done, given step 2.

Example:

1. $x = 5$, $y = 7$, then $N = 35$.
2. $(x - 1)(y - 1) = 4 \times 6 = 24$, so choose $p = 5$.
3. $s = 5$, since $ps = 25 = 1$ (modulo-24).

Applying this example we shall encode the 'message' 4:

$$E_p(4) = 4^5 \quad (\text{modulo-}35)$$

$$= 9$$

Table 8.1   Powers of K^5 modulo 35

	0	1	2	3	4	5	6
0	0	1	32	33	9	10	6
1	7	8	4	5	16	17	13
2	14	15	11	12	23	24	20
3	21	22	18	19	30	31	27
4	28	29	25	26	2	3	34

$$D_s(9) = 9^5 \quad \text{(modulo-35)}$$

$$= 4$$

A full table of powers of K^5 modulo 35 is given in Table 8.1. The table is clearly very trivial, partly because N is small, partly because $p = s = 5$, so that it is merely a table of an 'involution'. In a more serious application x and y would be very large, perhaps 100 digits each. It is not feasible to calculate x and y given N only; so it is not feasible for someone given N and p to calculate s. ('Not feasible' means that it would take centuries of computing, using known algorithms, to obtain the result.)

We conclude with a brief explanation of the theory behind the RSA approach.

There is a theorem by Fermat which states that:

$$K^{x-1} = 1 \quad \text{(modulo-}x) \tag{8.9}$$

if x is prime and K is not divisible by x

Now $D_s(E_p(K)) = D_s(K^p(\text{modulo-}N)) = K^{ps}(\text{modulo-}N)$.
But

$$K^{ps} = K^{a(x-1)(y-1)+1} \qquad \text{(by step 2 above)}$$

$$= 1 \times K(\text{modulo-}x) \qquad \text{(by Equation 8.9)}$$

Similarly

$$K^{ps} = 1 \times K(\text{modulo-}y)$$

Therefore

$$(K^{ps} - K) = 0(\text{modulo-}x) = ix$$

$$= 0(\text{modulo-}y) = jy$$

Since x and y are primes, i must be divisible by y, and j by x. In short:

$$K^{ps} - K = bxy = 0(\text{modulo-}N)$$

Therefore

$$K^{ps} = K(\text{modulo-}N)$$

Thus the original message K is retrieved after encrypting it (K^p) and then decrypting the encrypted message, $(K^p)^s$.

8.4 Conclusion

The brief review of data communications in this book begins with considering the physical problems of sending digital information serially over long distances. This involves discussing modems and line adaptors. But data transmission is subject to error, and one end of the line does not automatically know what is happening at the other end: line procedures are necessary, and these are discussed in Chapters 3 and 4. In turn line procedures need to be programmed (Chapter 5).

At this stage it becomes clear that communicating between computers is expensive in terms of lines, interfacing equipment and software. It is therefore of interest to put as much traffic through the infrastructure, in which one has invested, as possible: hence multiplexing (Chapter 6). One would also like to extend the coverage as much as possible, which implies networking. We have, in this book, discussed only passive networks: how they work, and what further facilities they imply. These are particularly obvious in the case of satellite networks where the need for error correction on reception and for encryption is plain. This final Chapter 8 discusses these two rather specialized topics, which are nonetheless very relevant to the future of data communications.

References

1. *APOLLO System Requirements Specification.* European Space Agency ESA SP-1068.

2. *Standard 802-4.* IEEE.

3. 'The performance of the satellite bridge in the Universe Project', A. Gillian Waters. In: *Performance of Computer-Communication Systems*, Rudin and Bax (eds.). North-Holland, Amsterdam, 1983.

4. *Error-Correcting Codes*, Wesley Peterson. Massachusetts Institute of Technology Press, Cambridge, MA, and John Wiley, New York.

   Two more recent books on coding are:
   Basics of Communications and Coding, W. G. Chambers. Oxford University Press, Oxford;
   Error-Control Techniques for Digital Communication, A. M. Michelson and A. H. Levesque. John Wiley, New York.

5. 'Convolutional codes and their performance in communication systems', A. J. Viterbi, *IEEE Transactions on Communications Technology*, October 1971.

6. A very readable book on encryption is *Security for Computer Networks*, D. W. Davies and W. L. Price, John Wiley, New York, 1984.

7. 'Federal Information Processing Data Encryption Standard', *Federal Register (USA)*, March 17, 1975 (*40 FR 12134*).

8. 'Encryption techniques for use on the British Telecom SatStream Service', S. C. Serpell and C. B. Brookson, *Br. Telecom Technol. J.*, July 1984, **2** (3).

9. 'New directions in cryptography', W. Diffie and M. Hellman, *IEEE Transactions on Information Theory*, IT-22, No. 6, November 1976.

10. *A Method for Obtaining Digital Signatures and Public-Key Cryptosystems*, R. Rivest, A. Shamir and L. Adleman. Massachusetts Institute of Technology Press, Cambridge, MA, April 1977.

Appendix Data interface on 25-pin D-type connector

D-type pin	CCITT V24 circuit	RS232-C circuit	Source	Description
1	—	AA	—	chassis ground
2	103	BA	T	Transmitted Data
3	104	BB	M	Received Data
4	105	CA	T	Request To Send (RTS)
5	106	CB	M	Clear To Send (CTS)
6	107	CC	M	Data Set Ready (DSR)
7	102	AB	—	common return (signal ground)
8	109	CF	M	Data Carrier Detect (DCD)
9	—	—	—	*
10	—	—	—	*
11	126	—	T	select transmit frequency*
12	122	SCF	M	backward channel DCD
13	121	SCB	M	backward channel CTS
14	118	SBA	T	backward channel Transmitted Data
15	114	DB	M	transmitted data clock
16	119	SBB	M	backward channel Received Data
17	115	DD	M	received data clock
18	141	—	T	initiate local analogue loopback
19	120	SCA	T	backward channel RTS
20	108/1	—	T	Connect Data Set to Line (CDSL)
	108/2	CD	T	Data Terminal Ready (DTR)
21	140	—	T	initiate remote digital loopback
	—	CG	M	signal quality indicator
22	125	CE	M	Ring Indicator (RI)
23	111	CH	T	data rate selector*
24	113	DA	T	external transmitted data clock*
25	142	—	M	test indicator

* Reserved for national use; may be assigned to different function by local P & T authority.

    pin 9: sometimes used as source of positive test voltage

    pin 10: sometimes used as source of negative test voltage

    pin 11: circuit 126 only used on V21 modems

source of signal:

    T = terminal or computer (DTE)

    M = modem (DCE)

Glossary

This glossary attempts to explain, in plain English, terms used in the text. For a more extensive, and perhaps more official, list of definitions of many terms the reader is referred to Fascicle X.1 of the CCITT *Red Book* (1985).

Acoustic coupler   A device for transforming digital signals into analogue waveforms suitable for transmission on a telephone (voice) circuit, and vice versa, and onto which the handpiece of a telephone may be mounted so that the transmitter 'speaks' into the mouthpiece and the receiver 'listens' at the earpiece. An acoustic coupler fulfills the function of a (low-speed) modem, with an acoustic rather than an electrical connection to the telephone circuit.

Anisochronous transmission   A transmission process such that between any two significant instants (e.g. bits) in the same group (e.g. a character) there is always an integral number of unit time intervals. Between two significant instants located in different groups, there is not always an integral number of unit intervals.

Arbitration Unit   An arbitration unit on a bus (q.v.) determines which device connected to the bus may be given control of it, and gives the control to the chosen device. Devices that wish to gain control of the bus make a request to the arbitration unit.

Asynchronous transmission   A loose term usually employed to refer to stop-start transmission, which is a form of anisochronous (q.v.) transmission in which coded characters in an envelope of start and stop bits are sent at irregular intervals. When used to refer to modems it implies that the modems are unaware of the bit-rate, i.e. they are not synchronized with the line adaptor or with each other by means of common clocking.

Authentication   A procedure for ensuring that the recipient of a message can be assured that the message has been sent by the purported sender and has not been (maliciously) altered, analogous to signing a document.

Availability   The proportion of time during which the critical functions of a system are available for use, i.e. there is no system failure.

Backward Channel   A channel on which data may be sent in the reverse direction, and usually at a much lower rate, to the main flow on the forward channel. It is normally possible to use the backward and forward channels simultaneously.

Bandwidth   The range of frequencies which a channel (e.g. a voice channel) can usefully exploit for transmitting information. Many channels have a low as well as a high limit to their frequency range, i.e. they cannot send DC levels of voltage.

Baseband transmission A system of transmission in which information, encoded into suitable waveforms, is sent directly over a channel without having recourse to a carrier waveform and modulation thereof, such that at any time only one information signal can be present without disruption.

Baud-rate The rate at which symbols are sent over a channel. The baud-rate is not necessarily equivalent to the bit-rate (q.v.), since a single symbol may be used to encode more than one bit at a time.

Bit A binary digit, i.e. 0 or 1, the smallest quantity of information. Strictly speaking a bit is a binary unit of information, but we have reserved the term 'Shannon' for this.

Bit error rate (BER) The proportion of bits in error in a binary message or on a channel. A BER of 10^{-5} means that 1 bit in 10^5 is, on average, in error.

Bit-rate The rate at which bits are transferred across a channel, usually measured in bits per second (bps).

Buffer An area of storage in which data are temporarily held. A buffer is usually thought of as belonging to one owning process at a time. Process A may 'pass' a buffer to process B, thereby relinquishing A's ownership in favour of B.

Bus A common physical highway usually composed of several tens of parallel circuits to which computer devices are attached, and using which any pair (or sometimes more than two) may communicate at any given time.

Carrier A continuous, usually sinusoidal, signal sent over a communication channel, which can be modulated (q.v.) by an information signal on transmission. On reception the information signal is extracted from the carrier by demodulation.

Channel A communication path over which information may be sent. A single physical circuit, or indeed any suitable medium, may support more than one channel at a time (multiplexing, q.v.) using a suitable technique. The word channel is not necessarily to be interpreted as a physical circuit.

Circuit switching A technique used in networks, such as the telephone network, in which a continuous (electrical) path is established on demand between two, or possibly more, users or terminals for the duration of the call, over which communication may take place, and which is maintained until the connection is released.

Coding The representation of symbols (such as A, B, C, etc.) from a source in terms of strings of symbols, called 'codewords', from a restricted code alphabet (such as binary 1 and 0, or hexadecimal). Coding theory is concerned with efficient representation, so that the strings are no longer than necessary, and at the same time provide redundancy in the form of check digits, so that transmission errors may be detected and/or corrected easily on reception.

Conditioning The improvement of the electrical characteristics of a circuit, such as a telephone circuit, to meet some minimal criteria of quantity. See also 'Equalization'.

Convolutional code   A method of coding (q.v.) in which the check digits are inserted throughout the transmitted message, rather than at the end as in a block code; and in which the check digits are calculated not only from the immediate group of information symbols, but from one or more of the preceding groups.

Crossbar   A type of circuit switching (q.v.) mechanism, used in telephone exchanges. It makes use of contacts closed by spring-mounted 'fingers' operated by solenoids. There are some 'electronic' crossbar switches.

DCE or Data Circuit-Terminating Equipment   The piece of equipment, such as a modem (q.v.), which terminates a circuit leading to a (data) network at the user's end, and to which he connects his DTE (q.v.). The DCE will be installed at the user's premises.

DMA or Direct Memory Access   A technique whereby data may be transferred directly between a peripheral device (controller) attached to a computer and the memory, without passing through the central processor.

DTE or Data Terminal Equipment   A term used to designate the user's equipment, terminal or computer, when attached to a (data) network via a DCE (q.v.). DTE is the source or sink for all communication across the network.

Duplex   Two-way simultaneous transmission. In common parlance this is often called 'full-duplex'. The term 'half-duplex' is used to mean that two-way transmission is possible, but not simultaneously. 'Half-duplex' is, strictly speaking, two-way alternate transmission.

Echo   The receipt of transmitted information back at the sender's receiver due to reflection, deliberate or otherwise, in the communication path or from the remote destination. A computer may deliberately echo typed characters received from a terminal so that the sender can see them. A telephone circuit may erroneously echo transmitted signals due to mismatches in the circuit.

Encryption   The process of coding (q.v.) messages in such a way that only those authorized to understand them may be able to do so, by the process of encryption. Encryption and decryption often involve the use of keys (secret or public) to enable the encrypting and decrypting algorithms to function correctly.

Entropy   The average information (q.v.) content of a stream of symbols emitted by a source. A high value for entropy means a high information content.

Equalization   In a modem (q.v.), the process of compensating for the undesirable (electrical) characteristics of a communication circuit, so that the signals carried by that circuit may be correctly interpreted on reception. Equalizers essentially compensate for undesirable relative attentuation and group delay characteristics.

Executive   In the operating system of a computer the executive, or 'kernel', is the central portion which allocates the processor to tasks or processes (q.v.), which enables tasks to communicate with each other, and which provides basic facilities for handling input and output.

Facsimile   A method of transmitting printed, graphical or other information from a page of a document, by scanning the page and coding each point or picture element (pixel). For example, a black pixel could be coded as 1, a white pixel as 0. Facsimile (FAX) can also handle intermediate grades of grey, and indeed colour. Because of the large amount of data acquired by this technique, FAX requires channels of large capacity and compression of the data is desirable.

Failover   The process of transferring the operation of a system or part of a system from a (defective) piece of equipment to some alternative piece of equipment. Failover is, ideally, rapid and automatic.

Firmware   Programs, usually of a low level such as those concerned with input/output, which are permanently implemented in Read Only Memory (ROM) or equivalent.

Forward error correction   The correction of messages which have been corrupted in transit, on reception; as opposed to detecting the error and asking for a retransmission by the sender.

Frequency Division Multiplexing (FDM)   A process in which several simultaneous channels (q.v.) may be made available on a single circuit or other medium, by allocating to each channel a restricted portion of the frequency bandwidth available.

Frequency Shift Keying (FSK)   A method of sending digital signals over a circuit, such as a telephone circuit, by representing a 1 by one frequency, a 0 by another.

Full-duplex   See 'Duplex'.

Gateway   A device, whose essential functions are usually provided by software, for interfacing two networks. A gateway is sometimes called a 'bridge'. A gateway reformats and/or re-interprets the messages valid on one network to make them intelligible to the other, and vice versa.

Half-duplex   Two-way alternate transmission. See also 'Duplex'.

Hamming distance   The number of digit positions in which the corresponding digits of two binary words of the same length are different.

In-band signalling   In-band signalling occurs when a channel which is used to carry data is also used to convey signalling information, for example to establish or clear a call, rather than using a separate control channel.

Information   Technically, the information conveyed by a symbol (or event) is defined as $(-\log_2 p)$ where p is the probability of occurrence of the symbol. The unit of information is the Shannon. If only two possible symbols exist and they are equally probable they each convey one unit of information. Since they can then be encoded optimally using one binary digit each, a unit of information is often referred to as a 'bit' rather than as a 'Shannon'.

Interrupt   A signal which interrupts the flow of a program in a computer, forcing it to start some new program by transferring control usually to an 'interrupt handler' in the executive (q.v.). The source of an interrupt is usually external to the central processor, for example in a device controller, although interrupts can be generated by fault conditions in the processor. It is also possible to have interrupts by software – 'software interrupts'.

Isochronous A transmission process such that between any two significant instants there is always an integral number of unit intervals. In isochronous transmission there is a real or imaginary continuous and regular clock with which all significant events are synchronized.

Kernel See 'Executive'.

LAN See 'Local Area Network'.

Leased line A (telephone) line which provides a permanent connection between two, or more, DTEs (q.v.), by-passing the switches in the intervening network, made available to a user (or group of users) for his (their) exclusive use.

Line adaptor or line controller Also called 'Serial Line Interface'. An input/output controller in a computer which converts parallel data to serial (q.v.) form on output for transmission on a channel; and does the reverse on input. It also usually provides facilities for controlling devices such as a modem from the computer.

Local Area Network (LAN) A network extending over distances up to a few kilometres for interconnnecting computing and similar equipment. They are usually characterized by high bit-rates (q.v.), e.g. 10 million bps. Typically the technique used is that of broadcasting a message, which includes the desired destination address, and only the equipment which has that address is supposed to receive the message. Most LANs may be regarded as serial buses (q.v.).

Loopback The technique of routing a channel back to its source, so that all data transmitted are immediately received again. It is used to check the functioning of equipment, channels and software.

Microwave Electromagnetic radiation with wavelength in the range 1 cm to 30 cm used as a carrier (q.v.) for information.

Modem A particular form of DCE (q.v.) which provides a serial digital interface to the DTE (q.v.) and which terminates a telephone (voice) circuit. A modem converts digital signals to analogue ones suitable for transmission on the voice circuit, and vice versa. 'Modem' is short for 'modulator–demodulator'.

By extension, the term 'modem' is used for any equipment which transforms digital signals to analogue signals (and vice versa) for long-distance transmission over any suitable medium.

Modulation The process whereby an underlying carrier (q.v.) wave is modified by signals representing information. Demodulation is the reverse process: the extraction of the information signals from the carrier. Amplitude modulation modifies the amplitude of the carrier; phase modulation modifies the phase; frequency modulation modifies the frequency. An example of phase modulation (in which the information is *digital*) could be that of a constant 2400 Hz carrier whose phase is changed 1200 times per second: $+90°$ to represent a 0, $+270°$ to represent a 1.

Multidrop circuit A circuit from a central (controlling) DTE (q.v.) with branches to several subsidiary DTEs. The circuit is usually a leased line (q.v.). The central DTE is usually a computer.

Multimode   Having many modes of operation. When used of modems (q.v.), 'multimode' usually signifies that the modem can be configured to provide various combinations of channels and speeds, rather than a single channel at a fixed speed.

Multipair cable   A cable containing many pairs of telephone wires, i.e. circuits.

Multiplexer   A device which merges independent channels, each on its own circuit (or equivalent), onto a common single physical facility: i.e. it performs multiplexing (q.v.). The reverse process, demultiplexing, will normally be simultaneously supported by the multiplexer.

Multiplexing   The support of several simultaneous channels on a single physical facility, such as a circuit.

Multipoint connection   Any physical connection linking more than two DTEs (q.v.).

Network   A collection of channels, interconnecting several DTEs (q.v.), which in principle enables any DTE to communicate with any other. Networks may or may not have active switches in them.

Node   See 'Switch'.

Octet   A group of 8 bits.

Optical fibre   A very small-diameter glass rod through which low-powered light signals may be transmitted, and successfully detected at the remote end. Because light has a very high frequency ($\sim 10^{14}$ Hz), it permits rapid modulation when used as a carrier.

Packet   A block of data with appropriate header information, identifying the type of packet and what is to be done with it; as used in packet switching (q.v.).

Packet switching   A packet-switched network is a particular form of a network (q.v.) for carrying digital data. In packet switching, all traffic between DTEs is in the form of packets (q.v.). Packets are routed from source DTE, to node (q.v.), to another node, etc., until they reach their destination DTE. At each intermediate node the packet is entirely received and stored before forwarding to the next node (or DTE).

Page mode   A method of using the screen or a terminal in which it displays always a page of information. The source of information can be imagined as divided into discrete pages. The screen will never show parts of distinct pages at the same time.

Parallel transmission   The sending of related digital information simultaneously over parallel circuits, e.g. on a bus (q.v.).

Parity digit   A parity bit is an extra bit added to a group of bits to ensure that the number of 1s is all even (even parity) or possibly all odd (odd parity). This enables an error in any single bit of the group to be detected. Several check digits appended to a block of data are often referred to as 'generalized parity check digits'.

Power line carrier A technique for providing voice and similar communication channels on high-tension transmission networks for electrical power.

Primitive An operation which is indivisible. It has either not taken place or it has taken place; but, at least as seen by its user, it never is in process of taking place.

Process An activity in a computer which can proceed in parallel with other activities. For example, a process to analyse received transactions will be in parallel with the input and output of other transactions, and probably in parallel with the process which stores or archives transactions. 'Process' is equivalent to 'Task'.

PTT A generic term, indicating the public telecommunication authority of any country, commonly used in Europe.

Re-entrant code Code that is written in such a way that it may be used simultaneously by more than one process (q.v.). Effectively the processes share the code but have independent workspace (q.v.).

Scheduling In a computer, the process of deciding which process or task (q.v.) is to run next. The *scheduler* is the piece of code in the executive (q.v.) which performs this scheduling. A scheduler is sometimes called a 'dispatcher'.

Scrambler A device for 'randomizing' data to avoid undesirable repeated patterns. Scramblers are used in some modems (q.v.).

Scroll mode A method of using the screen of a terminal like a continuous piece of paper, in which the latest information is always written at the bottom, and the display is 'scrolled' upwards losing the old information at the top.

Semaphore An indicator, in software, in a computer which is common to two or more processes (q.v.), facilitating their orderly communication. Typically it indicates 'Stop' or 'Go' to any process accessing it – hence the name.

Serial communication Communication in which information (e.g. bits) is sent serially (i.e. one after the other) along a channel.

Silo A hardware device into which data are put at the 'top' and from which they are extracted at the 'bottom'. It is a first-in-first-out buffer store.

Simplex channel A channel permitting communication in one direction only.

Skew The phenomenon of unequal arrival at their destination of signals which were simultaneously transmitted on parallel channels, due to differing propagation characteristics of those channels.

Stack A last-in-first-out store in a computer. A stack can usually be built anywhere in memory, and has a pointer to its top, which moves up when something is added to, down when something is taken from the stack.

Start-stop transmission See 'Asynchronous transmission'.

Store-and-Forward A technique used in data communications whereby a block of data is completely received (stored) at one point, before passing it on to the next. See 'Packet switching'.

Switch   A location at which traffic is switched. This implies that more than two channels meet at the switch; and that a decision must be made, when traffic arrives on one channel, onto which channel it is then to be forwarded. A switch is also called an 'exchange' or 'node'.

Synchronous transmission   Transmission in which devices work in synchronism under control of common clocking, for example the two line adaptors (q.v.) and modems (q.v.) at each end of a synchronous line. This usually implies isochronous (q.v.) transmission, but not necessarily. For example there might be pauses of indeterminate length between A sending synchronously to B and then B sending synchronously to A.

Task   See 'Process'.

Telex   A public circuit-switched international telegraph network for interconnecting 50 baud terminals, consisting of keyboards and printers, for sending (switched) text messages.

Time Division Multiplexing (TDM)   A method of multiplexing (q.v.) in which each channel is given at regular or irregular intervals brief periods of time ('time-slots'), on a common facility, in which to transmit or receive information. Traffic on different channels is thus interleaved on the common facility (circuit).

Token passing   A procedure for controlling access to a shared facility, for example a common physical circuit of a LAN (q.v.), in which only the process or equipment in possession of the 'token' may use the facility. The token is passed around the interested parties, processes or equipments, according to some algorithm.

Transparency   A transparent connection is one through which any pattern of information can be passed without the fear that some pattern may be interpreted as a control signal to the connection itself (e.g. to terminate it).

Waveform   A short analogue pattern, for example of voltage against time, of distinctive shape.

Wideband   Wideband is a loose term used to describe channels (q.v.) capable of carrying frequencies or bit-rates of the order of 10^4 cycles or bits per second, or higher.

Workspace   The area of memory retained by a process (q.v.) to hold intermediate results and other temporary data created or used by the process when it is active.

Index